COMING OF AGE,
Liver Spots & All

COMING OF AGE,
Liver Spots & All

A HUMOROUS LOOK AT THE
WONDERS OF GETTING OLD

DON MARSH

Walrus Publishing | St. Louis, MO

Walrus Publishing
an imprint of Amphorae Publishing Group LLC
Saint Louis, MO 63116
Copyright © 2018 Don Marsh

For information, contact
Walrus Publishing at 4168 Hartford Street,
Saint Louis, MO 63116
www.amphoraepublishing.com

Manufactured in the United States of America
Cover Design by Kristina Blank Makansi
Cover image courtesy of St. Louis Public Radio
Photo Credit: David Kovaluk, St. Louis Public Radio

Library of Congress Control Number: 2018936799
ISBN: 9781940442228

This book is dedicated to everyone of a "certain age" who goes to bed fearful and wakes up grateful, Also, to their kids and grandkids, especially those who have not yet taken away the car. May this book help them understand us better.

CONTENTS

Preface

This rambling account is primarily from a man's perspective, which, of course, makes it suspect. I am allowing myself to make certain assumptions about what older women feel. I have to, because every time I broach the subject of aging with women of a certain age and how they feel about the problems therewith, they say they don't want to talk about it. But, I *do* want to talk about it. So, I'll have to assume that many of my observations—some personal, some anecdotal—apply to them too. If they don't, well, they can write their own damn book.

Aging is a remarkable process. It is at once terrifying and interesting. Terrifying because it is a journey in which the ultimate destination is death. Interesting because of the destination. And, because of the journey to reach that end. Another aspect of that destination is that life is especially interesting near the end of that journey. Even when trying to think of this somewhat poetically, as in one of my favorite poems. Actually, it's one of my own poems. Which, like most of my writing, is unpublished. Until now. So, here's one for you.

Lengthening Shadows

The walk—the long and short of it—nears the end
As the sun dips just beyond the reach of the leafless trees.
Their bony branches reach toward the golden plate
While I watch my shadow, alongside, lengthen
Ahead of me on the manicured lawn.

I stop for a moment, and it stops, too.
Neither of us is in a hurry.

The only movement is an imperceptible one
As the already long shadow inches longer.
I wave at myself to see if it's really me
And then fasten the top button on
A well-worn coat just to make sure as a chill rakes over me.
I trod on. But then, slow down.
I'm in no hurry to reach the destination.
The terminus … with no return.

But then I resume my journey. One never to repeat.
Even if I find ways to change my route and extend my trip.
My arrival is as inevitable as it is final.

No place to hide.
No turning back.
No bargaining.

As I turn the final corner, I again slow.
My shadow, too.
Only it reaches out well ahead of me as if mocking my pace.
My only consolation: it will arrive well before I do.
But, in turn, I, too, will be erased by the oncoming darkness.
Or is that a light I see?

So much for the terrifying.
And the interesting.
They are both connected. Besides, what could be more interesting than getting the answer to the ultimate questions about life after death? Heaven and hell? And that damn light at the end of the tunnel?

The truth is that the final years—those years of lengthening shadows—are in and of themselves, both interesting and terrifying. At times, one's mind becomes a bit undependable; one wonders about outliving one's resources. And, the body changes physically.

Body changes include changes in health. Take it from someone who is 78 as of this writing, and who has had open heart surgery and prostate surgery. Toss in cataract surgery for bonus points. What could be more terrifying and interesting than all of that? Even so, I am not an expert on aging, other than I have managed to navigate life successfully.

So far. But check back tomorrow.

So, what I'm (we're) trying to do here is whistle past the cemetery, not literally, of course, but at least figuratively. And, to talk about the realities of coming-of-old age with some advice, and some added humor, in hopes the older folks will nod and smile with understanding and recognition, and that younger folks will understand a little better what we're going through, have gone through, and what we have yet to go through.

So, as we embark on this project, I offer this—

Advice
There comes a time when an old man is asked
to pass along the wisdom life has lent.
There is none.
For one man's perception of what is wise
may very well be folly to the next.
But the worst of burdens to carry to the last
is the rucksack weighed down with rocks of regret.
So many things one might have done.
So many things deferred and then never done.
Excuses. So many.
Regrets. So many.
So, then, what is wise?
Perhaps it is *not* to allow yourself to be put in the position

of saying "I wish I had done that!" It might be a good idea to begin with a little test. First, to determine if you are officially old.

Can you identify the following without cheating?

- Tojo
- Joseph Welch
- Christine Jorgensen
- Fran Allison
- 38th parallel
- Brace Beemer
- John L. Lewis
- Ted Mack
- *Señor* Wences
- Joe Btfsplk
- *Collier's Magazine*

Know many or most of them? If so, let's face it. You are officially old.

What about these?

- Anatoli Dobrynin
- Adam Clayton Powell
- Yuri Gagarin
- Charles Manson
- John Cameron Swayze
- Hunter S. Thompson
- Me Lai
- Hyannis Port
- Dr. Strangelove

- Bates Motel

If you know most, or at least many in this list, retirement for you is most likely in

the near future. Here's one more.

- The Challenger
- Windows
- World Series Quake
- Mikhail Gorbachev
- Cell phones
- Bhopal
- Exxon Valdez
- Apple
- Linda Tripp
- Run-D.M.C.

Okay, so, here's the thing: if you know about most in the above list (I even know who Run-D.M.C is. Yeah, yeah. I had to Google him … it … whatever), you should be reading this book so that you understand the people who nailed the previous questions better than you did.

Now, the final test.

- Al Gore
- http://
- "Mission Accomplished"
- Apps
- Lady Gaga
- Twittter
- Arab Spring

- Friending
- *Fifty Shades of Grey*
- Podcasts (do you get the feeling there's a theme embedded in the list?)

If you had no trouble identifying the topics and people in this last group, you may laugh and think, "Retirement? That's light years away!" Well, that's the same thing I said in my twenties, too. Only, now, I'm not laughing.

One more thing: if you were able to add a checkmark next to the names or things in *all* the categories above, you must be of very sound mind. And hopefully, sound body. Nonetheless, I'd like to remind you to remember the old adage, 'Here today, gone tomorrow,' So, don't forget to get your affairs in order. Now.

Moving right along. … The chapters that follow were randomly considered and presented. And, there is no particular logic to the order in which these subjects were presented.

The first subject might be an unusual way to get into all this old business, but, how we look and how we feel—at least at this age—are a couple of things most of us think about, worry about, and wonder about.

So, here we go.

Introduction

Getting old isn't for sissies. So, I'll be brief. Why? Because the sands of time are racing way too fast. Secondly, um, I've forgotten the other thing. Except … getting old isn't for sissies.

1: Liver Spots & Bruises

Okay, so where do we start?

Honestly, there are so many starting points that I have already wasted way too much time thinking about it. So, I figured, why not just go with "liver spots." Don't wrinkle your nose. It happens. Besides, as a writer, I've been taught to "write what you know." And I know about liver spots. Every time I've sat down to write this book, I see them staring back at me as my fingers rest on the computer keys. And each day, they've brought along a new friend. Bastards.

Don't get me wrong. It's not that I'm vain. I consider liver spots an intellectual challenge. Where do they come from? Why don't they go away? And why does the dog insist upon licking them? In fact, why does the dog insist upon licking anything? Especially after giving the neighbor's Shih Tzu's butt a nice once-over, or immediately after taking a nice drink from the toilet. In fact, why the dog does these sorts of things is as difficult a question to answer as where liver spots come from.

I note that no less a formidable institution than the Mayo Clinic calls them "age spots," which I think I like even less. These little beauties are also called "solar lentigines." If I could pronounce that, it might be my preferred choice of phrases. That way, no one would know what I was talking about. However, being the intellectual sort that I am, I think therein lies a clue. Solar! So, they have something or the other to do with the sun. And I thought that the brown coating compliments of the sun was called a "tan." Mea culpa. Okay, okay, I do suppose it's hard to make a case that fifty spots randomly dotting the back of my hands—some the size of a dime, some smaller, some larger—could be called a tan. Tans are something acquired at the beach or in a tanning bed. I don't go to the beach, and I don't frequent tanning beds. Besides, have you ever heard of a "liver spot bed," or, better yet, a "solar lentigines bed?" Me neither. And in all of this, complicating the issue is that sometimes the spots are black!

In my case, as is the case with many of my contemporaries, the initial appearance (usually around age 50) of solar lentigines … oh, what the hell … liver spots … causes one to wonder if these spots are skin cancer. (Unfortunately, no pretty alternative for that phrase.) Once again, however, the Mayo Clinic comes to the rescue with the reassuring observation that it is not skin cancer. Unless, of course, it is.

More reassurances come with word from Google that there are any number of bleaching products on the market to lighten liver spots. There is a downside to that, though. While the likely outcome is that those solar lentigines will go away, they'll merely be replaced by a nifty little pinkish spot—about the size of a dime ... or smaller ... or bigger.

The choice is clear. One can choose to keep the solar lentigines, er, liver spots, and engage in a friendly competition with peers: "Ha! I have more than you have!" Or, go for the bleach and risk looking like a character from *Where the Wild Things Are*.

Then there's the question as to *why* they are called "liver spots" There is no consensus here, that I can find, although some suggest that it's because they are the same color as the liver. Not any liver I have ever seen at the butcher shop. (As an aside, I refer to a "butcher shop," which is a phenomenon largely unknown in twenty-first century America, having been replaced by the "meat section" in the local supermarket.) There is also another speculation that early elders thought these stunners might have been caused by liver problems. That, I believe, is very much in doubt. Anything I'm aware of caused by the liver usually presents in some variation of the color yellow, which could be caused by any number of things not necessarily related to age. But, I digress. So, let's move on.

As if these liver spots aren't bad enough, there is another side to these age-old ... old age blemishes: blood spots. Which are in direct competition with our liver spots. You see, some of us take blood thinners. It's not that we necessarily think that our blood is fat, or that we're trying to look svelte, it's usually because our cardiologist has told us that not taking them could be fatal. Why? Irregularity. No, not that kind. The heartbeat kind, which can cause serious problems. It seems a skipped beat or two can cause blood to pool in the heart. I'm not sure exactly where in the heart that pooling could take place, because when Doc said "fatal," I couldn't take those pills fast enough.

No, it's not on the list of my favorite things to do every day. But that little pill lessens the chances of coagulation, which lessens the possibility of a stroke.

The drawback here is that any part of the body—especially hands, arms, legs, also are susceptible to bruising. So, not only are there brown liver spots to deal with, there are also nice, dark blue spots, which eventually change into a rainbow of stormy colors: purplish black, reddish yellow, and pukey green. And they are usually much bigger, which, on the bright side, overshadows those pesky brown spots.

The key here is to avoid anything with claws. Dogs for instance. My relative's dogs seem attracted to me, and often rake their claws along my arms and hands as I reach out to give them treats. Admittedly, they are a bit more aggressive when I don't give them treats. On second thought, maybe they just dislike me. Or maybe it's the old person smell. Yes, I've been told there is an old person smell. Of course, I've never detected it, though I did have an uncle who had a smelly problem. What I call a young person's smell involves sneakers.

At any rate, it's best to steer clear of anything with claws if you want to lessen your chances of adding another range of colors to your body. They do go away, however. Eventually.

We could get into another discussion of old folks and "spotting", but that seems inappropriate here. But you know what I mean.

2: Millennials

Millennials. You know who they are. They're young, 18-34, in their prime, with at least one dog—and tattoos. Many live in a basement near you. Perhaps very near. Perhaps in your basement. Does the word "boomerang" have any resonance?

I have relatives who are Millennials, and they share many of the same values as I do. So, it's not that I dislike them. Maybe a better word is envy. On the one hand, there are now more of them than there are baby boomers. I'm pre-baby boomer, the so called "Silent Generation." We don't have the same multi-tasking skills of the millennials who can text while walking through Best Buy, riding a bike or, shudder, while driving at sixty miles an hour on a crowded highway. All the while they hit the right characters on their phone key-pads. These are skills to be admired … or feared. And, they do this with their thumbs!

And, they are very good at social media.

And, they are especially good at letting everyone with a front row ticket to the cyber world stay up to date. They are willing scribes of the hourly play by play of what they are watching, eating, drinking, or where they are at any given time. And, with attached photos to prove it!

They are also very good at showing their contempt for elders, at least those who disavow texting, Facebook, YouTube, Flickr, Tumblr, and Instagram, not to mention any other digital resource invented since I began writing this sentence.

Plus, they are experts at finding unusual apps and immediately understanding how they work. (If you don't know what an app is, Google it.)

They will lobby long and hard to convince you that Bitcoin is the new gold standard, and that Uber is the only way to go. Or come.

They are good at taking every minute of accrued vacation time and are less inclined to vote than their parents or grandparents.

They are very good at returning home to live with mom and dad after encountering any bumps in the road. Or before. Research by the respected Pew Research Center shows that for the first time in 130 years, Millennials are more likely to be living at home with parents than they are to be living with a spouse or partner in their own place. It's a slight difference. Less than one percent, but it is still very close to one third of the Millennial population, overall, our largest demographic group. Interestingly, that's almost exactly half of what the number was in the sixties. You remember the sixties. Or do you?

In today's world, under the worst possible scenarios, they may return with young children, perhaps with a one-sided yarn about miscommunication, incompatibility, and suspicions or proof of infidelity.

And, as aforementioned, they come fully accessorized with at least one dog, perhaps two, and they might even bring along a cat, ensuring that anyone with pet dander allergies will push up the price of Benadryl stock.

It remains to be seen how good they'll be at paying off student loans, not to mention how much they'll have left over to help defray our nursing home costs.

But, they are smart, and apparently have good instincts on social issues, such as racism and gay rights.

They may be lacking in patience and thereby feeding a voracious appetite for resentment on one important front: Jobs. Almost 70 million Baby Boomers are ahead of them in line on the jobs front. Boomers hold the better jobs on the employment ladder, thereby allowing Millennials to stack up on the lower rungs, jabbing elbows at each other, while bemoaning the lack of movement above.

Boomers are working longer and taking their sweet time going into retirement mode (see retirement). This is likely to get worse before it gets better (see Mortality). Millennials, as I have said, are smart. One way they are finding to work around the job issue is by developing important entrepreneurial skills. That is, "If you can't join 'em …" Thus they are creating thousands of new businesses along with millions of jobs. More often than not, these new enterprises have high tech, digital world components.

Actually, this is an ingenious form of "get even." In other words, creating a world in which those of us at the top of the ladder find it increasingly difficult to function effectively. I suspect they are also waiting to get even with us for having to clean up the mess we are leaving them. What we may not be leaving them is a financially viable Social Security account when they reach retirement age. Fact is, we're just living too long (check your local dictionary for the definition of "mortality"). However, we have our reasons. Another reason to lock the basement door and windows at night.

###

* The term "senior" is bothersome to many older people. When I was a senior in high school I had something to look forward to. When I was a senior in college, I had a career to look forward to. As a "senior" in life, I have only eternal oblivion to look forward to.

So, let's look for something with a more encouraging and positive connotation. I've always thought "second childhood" would work a little better.

3: Gravity

With apologies to Sir Isaac Newton, I hate gravity. He didn't invent it. But he put it on the map. Galileo and Albert Einstein also played roles, but as sure as an apple will fall down, not up, it's Newton who gets the starring role in my gravity movie (not the one starring Sandra Bullock and George Clooney, each of whom is approaching an age in which gravity will play a starring role in their lives).

What is gravity? It's called the weakest of the fundamental actions of nature. Don't ask me what the others are. It might make me more depressed than I already am.

Back to Newton. Here's how Wikipedia explains it.

"In 1687, English mathematician Sir Isaac Newton published *Principia*, which hypothesizes the inverse-square law of universal gravitation." In his own words, "I deduced that the forces which keep the planets in their orbs must [be] reciprocally as the squares of their distances from the centers about which they revolve: and thereby compared the force requisite to keep the Moon in her Orb with the force of gravity at the surface of the Earth; and found them answer pretty nearly."

Got it? Yeah, me, too.

Forget the talk of orbs and inverse square laws.* I'm talking boobs and chins and jowls, and those muffin tops that peek ... or sometimes explode exponentially over the beltline. Of course, I must not forget to mention that part of the upper arm that gets increasingly flabby each time the earth circles the sun. Yes, this is the science part of my spiel.

Gravity is indeed the culprit. Falling hair. Drooping eyelids. That under-the-chin thing that plunges like a goiter in hot pursuit of what I do not know.

There doesn't seem to be much that can be done naturally to stop all this. But there is an inclination to call the nearest plastic surgeon. Which many do. I've not given in to this calling—what I call the growth industry—yet. Funny thing, though, the irony of this growth industry is not lost to me. Now, instead of removing things, the object is to make things smaller, pull them back up, zap them with a laser.

However, it has been suggested that some of these flaws (my word) can be corrected by, of all things, diet and exercise. Besides, most of us are already on a diet of some sort. More often than not, it has something to do with controlling cholesterol. Which brings up the issue of good versus bad cholesterol. I don't know about you, but that is as difficult for me to understand, much less explain, as hypothesizing the inverse-square law.*

And this diet usually involves something super nutritious that is soft or liquid and sometimes tasteless. Or green and tasteless, and to stray from this healthy menu item might do one considerable harm (see Mortality). Maybe. Even so, give me something that is crunchy and full bodied with lots of cheese and sauces any old day. (But again ... see Mortality.)

I do admit to a certain skepticism that *any* diet has *any* chance of stopping gravity's inexorable mission, no matter what the doctor says. The mission of Newton's Law, aside from making us weep, is to drag us down into misshapen and unrecognizable beings. Thank goodness, the process is gradual and people who see us every day don't notice it so much at first. Until one day, when the inevitable occurs and Newton's Law, which has been stalking us, says, "OK folks, it's time to let it all hang out." Then fifty-year-old Bob and Betty, with a sideways cock to their heads bemoan, "Poor Joe, or Poor Maude. I never noticed those bags under her eyes, or that paunch that hides his belt. Age sure creeped up on them." Creeped. Hell, it landed with a slam dunk. The one consolation is that the same thing is happening to them, too.

One thing about the gravity mission, though, is that it has a fashion component in that it calls for frequent wardrobe adjustments. Not the taking-in kind, but the letting-out kind.

Then again, there is always exercise those snotty-nosed fifty-year-old kids say.

Yeah, right.

Don't you know I've got a bad heart? Why do you think they put me on that crappy diet? I'll take the sagging chin, flabby upper arms, and sagging breasts, any old day (Again … see Mortality). Besides, between me and you, they just want my social security check.

Even so, if you have submitted to trying to re-sculpt your pitiful body, there are a few things to keep in mind. Even when a doctor encourages moderate exercise along with the diet, if he or she encourages anything more complicated than walking, then this is akin to a death sentence, and what he or she is attempting is trying to kill you. Maybe they want your social security check, too? Or maybe the attempted homicide may be the result of an old invoice waiting to be paid, or, since we older folks are now living longer, maybe it involves new Congressional attempts to reduce Medicare benefits. In that case, if you are on Medicare, it's Congress that's trying to put you into an early grave (see Mortality).

This can all be sliced and diced to death (see Mortality). However, there are certain words that come to mind in this discussion. And they all contain the letter 'G': Gravity. Pulmonary ConGestion. StaGnation of the blood. Grave (see Mortality).

Grave. That's the worst one. Gravity in what may be its most dangerous state. The word brings to mind another aspect of gravity. Falling ... falling. There I've said it again. Aside from drawing that last breath and looking for that supposed light at the end of that dark tunnel (are we to believe that the road to heaven is actually through a tunnel?), there are few things that also terrify us about falling. Broken hips, broken pelvises, even a broken arm can lead to the end of the road ... and to the tunnel. And don't even think about a fractured skull. Too often, the accident, assuming you did not fall intentionally, leads to bed rest and extended inactivity. That, in turn, can lead to a condition called hypostatic pneumonia. Another scary word *without* a 'G'.

Thusly defined, according to Merriam-Webster, hypostatic pneumonia.is "Pulmonary congestion due to the stagnation of blood in the dependent portions of the lungs in old persons or in those who are ill and lie in the same position for long periods." Which leads me to "stagnation of blood." I thought as long as we were breathing, our blood was circulating through our bodies. Guess not. So, what does that mean, really? Really, I don't think I want to know. One thing I do know, if one acquires hypostatic pneumonia, your bed is a good place to be. Of course, you don't want to stay there too long, stagnation of the blood and all. Otherwise, well, you know....

Before we leave the issue of gravity, I want to address something. Why is it that our ears and noses GROW larger as we get older? I read in one of those newspaper doctor columns, that that particular doctor insists they do not. It's only an optical illusion. Optical illusion or not, I swear my nose and ears have optical-illusioned themselves by about twenty percent.

If the good doctor's wrong, and they have been known to be on occasion, maybe it's like the other flab. But I don't normally associate the ears and nose with flab. Yet, they do seem to grow. If they do, and if gravity were in control, why don't they just drop below the jaw and chin? This is a puzzlement. Is it contrary to the laws of physics (or physiques)? Unfortunately, we second childhood types, only have limited time to come up with answers. Maybe the doctor's right. I'll leave it to the Millennials to figure it out. But, of course, they won't give it a thought for a few decades.

*For those who want the inverse-square law explained, Wikipedia does it this way:

In physics, an inverse-square law is any physical

law stating that a specified physical quantity or intensity is inversely proportional to the square of the distance from the source of that physical quantity. The fundamental cause for this can be understood as geometric dilution corresponding to point-source radiation into three-dimensional space (see diagram). Mathematically formulated as a constant quantity:

$$\text{intensity}_1 \times \text{distance}_1^2 = \text{intensity}_2 \times \text{distance}_2^2$$

It can also be mathematically expressed as: The divergence of a vector field which is the resultant of radial inverse-square law fields with respect to one or more sources is everywhere proportional to the strength of the local sources, and hence zero outside sources. Newton's law of universal gravitation follows an inverse-square law, as do various other phenomena.

That should teach you to temper your curiosity. (You may notice that I often use and reference Wikipedia. That is simply to show you that I am computer literate. And lazy.)

4: Retirement

In one of my first jobs, I can remember the visit to (what would now be called the Human Resources (HR) office). Then, HR was the boss's secretary. All the necessary business was completed with her, and I was advised that my anticipated retirement date was forty-five years from my next birthday. I laughed out loud. Forty-five years! My God, that was not only in the next century, it was literally in the next millennium. There was no way that that day could ever come. Forty-five years! No way. Of course, it did. And then it was if it had all taken a very short forty-five minutes.

This leads me to one thing. If there is one constant in life, it's time. Contrary to when I was a kid, time now clicks along at an alarming rate. Then, time slowed to a crawl—at least during school and those long, horrid winter months—and in the dentist's chair. It moved considerably faster when I was making out in the back of the family car. But I digress. Yes, I know: a second is a second, an hour is an hour, and a day is a day, ,and days turn into months, months into years. And somewhere along the line, it does skip a beat. In Leap Year. So, does that mean I've lost a day or gained a day closer to reaching that damned tunnel?

But hopefully, before then, comes retirement. Retirement. A lovely word. Every working person's dream. Right? Well, now, I'm reminded of the phrase, "Be careful what you wish for, you just might get it."

Retirement is not as easy as it sounds, or all it's cracked up to be. Especially if you can't do it because China's economy keeps taking swipes at the 401-K. But, that's a story for another day.

Recently, I was at Sam's to pump some discounted gas (See Parsimony), and ran into a former colleague, who was now in his seventies. Retired. He came around the island of pumps and came up short when he saw me. He was wearing one of those little red aprons. You know them as telltale sign to look for when one needs some help, which most days now, when one *really* needs some assistance, seems to be nonexistent. We're lucky to find one of those well-hidden buttons to push and wait for the overhead speaker to address our needs. At any rate, when we met, he apparently, having been a successful salesman during his entire career, was embarrassed. I guess he felt he had to explain his presence to me.

"We traveled around the world and did everything else we ever wanted to do. So, after drumming up things to do—and doing them—sometimes twice ... and more, I woke up one morning and realized our bucket list was fulfilled, and that there are 365 days to a year. After that, I got bored. And now, here I am. I'm not bored anymore; I get to see and talk with people every day. Now, I've got purpose again."

Another older friend was a golf nut and had looked forward to playing every day. After about a year of retirement and his heavily senior discounted rounds, I joined him at one of the local courses. He played like crap, which made it a highly competitive round. "So," I asked him, "do you enjoy playing every day?"

He shrugged his shoulders. "It's great," he said. "But I really don't care how well I play anymore, because I know I'll be out again tomorrow."

In other words, his passion for the game was gone. Less than a year later he was too. He keeled over on the thirteenth green.

With this, it has been my observation that people who retire, and who have no real plan or purpose, aren't long for this world.

Seems that red apron is not a bad alternative after all.

For those of us who do survive, however, there is another downside. Not for the man. For his wife. While the husband spent thirty or forty years heading off to work every day, many wives (at least back in my day), stayed home, raised the kids, kept the house ship-shape, lunched with friends, shopped, volunteered and otherwise kept the entire family running like a well-oiled machine.

Then, he retires. And not only does his life change drastically, so does hers. Except, her work and routine haven't. But because the old man is underfoot now, her schedule has to conform to his. It's no longer lunch with the ladies; it's making lunch for him. It's no longer the hairdressers at mid-morning; it's listening to him read the obituaries … out loud.

His life may be one of pleasant leisure. Hers has become one of manic desperation.

Too old for divorce. Suicide is out of the question. Homicide, however, is an option, as my wife once told me when I decided to try my hand at cooking. But of course, she knows it's a temptation better resisted. Funny thing, I found a book titled, *How to Commit the Perfect Crime* nestled in my chair the other day. My wife swore she had no idea where that came from.

It is these wives who pray that he will take up golf or fishing. Or put on one of those red aprons.

So, there you have it. When you see a group of gentlemen retirees playing cards or checkers in the local park, or outside the courthouse, or sitting at the bar of the local tavern, you'll understand.

5: Stuff

One fallout of longevity is acquiring stuff. If you doubt that, try moving after a few decades at one address. Why does it become increasingly difficult to throw things away as we get older? Is it a deep-seeded fear that discarding things we once felt valuable is symbolic of how society will look upon us as we get older and more feeble? Or that, God forbid, our kids or grandkids will one day put us in storage. It happens.

We hang on to old clothes, personal artifacts, pictures and other memorabilia with the mistaken notion that surviving family members will find them as valuable as we once did. But really, why cling to that autographed photo of Phil Rizzuto, or the third-grade report card, not to mention that old Sigma Phi Epsilon fraternity paddle?

The kids don't want that crap. It means nothing to them. And, truth be known, the very first thing they will do when the time comes, is toss it. Save them the trouble.

Do it now! Hard as it may be to deep-six eight track tapes and 45 RPM records, they must go!

Even so, there are some things that are almost universally retained: old family photos, World War II army uniforms, old recipes, framed letters from once famous, or not so famous people, or Grandma's baby spoon. Rest assured, however, these will probably be the first things to go.

"Who's in this photo?" Bobby asks.

His sister grabs the pic and gives it a cursory glance and says, "Hell if I know."

In the trash it goes.

There is one thing that we might want to hold on to, though. Furniture. Yes, by the time we retire, the furniture has become a classic, perhaps even an antique. But many of us can't bring ourselves to get rid of our comfortable recliner with cigarette burns, holes, and stains from God knows where. The grandkids love it, too. Besides, home, as they say, is where the heart is—and the furniture. After all we do need someplace to sit, sleep, and eat, And by the time we are heading into that tunnel of light, we won't care if it does find its way to the Salvation Army. So there.

Now, having said that, I will be holding on to some of the things that have special significance. That autographed photo of Phil Rizzuto, my third grade report card, and that old Sigma Phi Epsilon fraternity paddle.

And, seeing the resurgence of interest by the Millennials and Gen X'ers, it would be foolish to get rid of those eight track tapes or those vintage 45 RPM records. By the time we kick the bucket, they could be worth millions. Really. (See Parsimony). Hell, remember Mickey Mantle's rookie card, the one you put on a clothes pin and attached to your bike's wheel spokes? Yeah, that one. That card is now worth somewhere north of $20,000. (FYI: Phil Rizzuto's card goes for a little over $100.)

6: The First Thing to Go

The aging process brings with it a series of transformations. We've already discussed gravity and the way it pulls us down into collapsing piles of adipose tissue. Somewhere along the way, we seem to rationalize, and come to accept that as inevitable. But some of the changes are less dramatic. Visibly, at least. And, at first no one notices but us. And some of us choose to ignore this.

At first, the vision issue usually comes when reading the paper. No, I don't mean to suggest that you will open the paper and find a story on page seven proclaiming that you are having vision issues. It's more like when you squint your eyes so tight to see if you are actually on page seven, or page nine. At first, it's easy to shrug that off with the facile and welcome conclusion that you are just tired and didn't sleep well the night before. And, because you are retired, it doesn't really make any difference if you are on the first page or the last. With all the time you have on your hands, you'll get to every page sometime during the day.

Of course, after weeks—maybe months—of this rationale, you realize that rubbing your eyes no longer helps. But the real tell-tale sign that maybe it's time to see that eye doctor, is when holding the paper at arm's length, or close to your nose, is no longer close enough or far enough away. Not only can you no longer make out the page numbers, you can't even make out any words. And eventually, someone else notices and finds it necessary to bring it to your attention.

"Honey," my wife says, "how can you see with that newspaper up against your nose? I think it's time we took you to the eye doctor."

"Nonsense. I can see just fine." What I didn't tell her was that in order to see the print, I have to hold the paper at arms length, or that, really, what I was doing was napping behind the newspaper.

In all of this, though, there is a natural inclination to wonder if publishers have reduced the size of the font from ten points to six points. Smaller font translates into fewer pages. That makes sense given the increasing cost of newsprint and shrinking newspaper profits—and perhaps that the CEO's are GenX'rs and can still see just fine, thank you very much. Our one consolation: they are next in line. Thank you very much.

So, we go to visit the ophthalmologist, our newfound

friend, who will do the requisite tests and prescribe glasses. Undoubtedly bifocals. Or, egads, even trifocals.

All goes well until he says, "You need cataract surgery."

"That's for old people," I say.

All the ophthalmologist does is raise his eyebrows.

One more confirmation that the clock is ticking.

Turns out, the surgery is not so bad. The required eye patch is actually quite dashing and invariably encourages expressions of compassion or variations on any of several dozen cyclops jokes.*

But all good things must come to an end, and within 24-48 hours, the compassion and frivolity passes. What is restored is improved vision. Amazingly, that vision is once again three-dimensional. Something that had been lost along the way so gradually, the patient hadn't even realized it. Bonus points to the surgeon. Bonus points to me for having the good sense to go to the doctor.

Of course, the realization that, along with the rest of our bodies, our vision is deteriorating is usually a gradual process. One doesn't wake up one day with a plethora of aches and pains, swelling at the ankles, or the overwhelming desire to sit down and proclaim, "Eureka! I'm a senior citizen." (a.k.a. in my second childhood). The same thing with our vision. Especially among men. Men have difficulty accepting things relating to reflections on their manhood and physical deterioration. Our macho-ness is comprised of denial, self-diagnosis, and the refusal of *any* suggestion we should seek professional diagnosis and treatment. *Who me?*

For many of us, that awareness comes as a slap in the face when we make a routine trip to Walgreens or CVS, to select a birthday card for our wife. After a few minutes of moving the card back and forth like we are rowing a boat, out of growing desperation, we go to the generic eyeglass case and try on a pair. After a few tries, there is that wonderful moment of discovery when you find that you can actually read the card you have in your hand. And you realize the card you selected reads: "Belated condolences on your loss." So, along with the card, you buy a pair of over-the-counter reading glasses. Eventually though, each time you go to CVS, you chuck a couple more pairs on the checkout counter. Like potato chips, you find you can't have just one. So, now they're stashed everywhere: the glove compartment, the golf bag, by your favorite chair, the bedside table, the kitchen counter, the shower. Yes, the shower. Heaven knows I don't want to mistake my wife's Nair for shampoo. Reading problem, solved.

Until you realize you can't see things at a distance. Like a well-driven golf ball. Or that person waving at you from across the restaurant calling your name like you are his best friend, or if that thing in the road ahead of you is a stopped car.

Then, and only then, do men think, "Honey, don't you

think it's time you had an eye exam? Of course, I'll go, too. For moral support, you know."

"Dad! Didn't you hear what I said?"

"Uh, no. I was reading the newspaper."

Then there's hearing loss. Also a gradual process, but it becomes a team sport before all is said and done. That's because the person with the problem soon becomes a problem for those around him. Especially wives and children.

Dad! Didn't you hear what I said?"

"Uh, no. I was reading the newspaper."

Another all-too-familiar phrase is, "What did you say?" And this isn't just while having a normal conversation, watching television or movies, or listening to the radio. It also happens during public announcements at airports and train stations. Or when someone's asking directions. Or telling you that the road ahead as been washed out. By then, it is much more than a nuisance. Especially when the person without a hearing problem seems obligated to respond in full voice—a.k.a., shout—to the utter displeasure of those within a full city block. Or those within normal hearing distance.

Hearing aids can help. But have you priced them recently? (See Parsimony) One must carefully weigh the expense against the frustration or animosity of those around you. Not only that, the vanity factor comes into play. People, both men and women, do not like to admit to aural frailty. Add to that having a mechanical device shoved into their ear—even in today's world of miniaturization—is not like wearing a pair of diamond earrings. But even worse, they usually signify that the wearer is someone who is *old*! What could be worse than that?

Well, I'm here to tell you. There is one thing that *is* worse. Memory loss … and the fear of spiraling downward to dementia, and worse … Alzheimer's. Who of any age doesn't worry about that? Even our younger set, I would say.

I think it's safe to say that we have all experienced memory loss at one time or another. Who hasn't forgotten the name of someone they've just met? Or, who among us has not walked into a room to get something and forgotten what it was we were looking for by the time we get there? That's always worth a good laugh. By others. That's another reason to keep a good supply of reading glasses handy.

Less humorous is the slippery slope of dementia/Alzheimer's beginning with mild cognitive issues affecting thinking, reasoning, and judgment. There's no humor there. Just dread.

As I said, getting old is not for sissies. And, like it or not, we eventually have to put our vanity in "time out."

###

* Example: If you're a teacher it must be easy having only one pupil.

7: What Is That Smell Anyway?

Old people get a bad rap. Let's talk about the sense of smell (note I resisted the temptation to write "scents" of smell, although I may use it later), or how they smell. Let's be clear. I mean my sense of smell. Not how I smell.

Let me give you an example. Some years ago, the satirical website *The Onion* wrote a news brief entitled, "Doctors No Closer to Cure For Old-Person Smell."

First, let me say that the Onion is a satirical online magazine, so the satire is tongue-in-cheek, and in this instance, they take on … well, here's the gist (or is it jest?) of the article, and I quote:

"Doctors at Johns Hopkins University announced … no progress has been made in the fight to cure Old-Person Smell. … But it is our solemn vow to lead the fight against this strange, kinda-stale smell … until no elderly person's family or friends have to experience that weird, sorta-medicinal, sorta-uriney odor ever again."

Of all the … "Kinda-stale," "sorta-medicinal," and "sorta-uriney" are not funny. So, my wrath is reserved for *The Onion* and the staffers who came up with all of this. Don't get me wrong, like so many, I'm a fan of satire, and granted, a lot of people, myself included, are willing to accept such headlines as, "Dad's Eyes Light Up at the Sight of a Perfectly Packed Cooler." Or, "Thirteen-Year-Old Drinking Prodigy Accepted by Ohio State." I can certainly relate to the first, and know very well that if a kid is not a drinking prodigy, he can go to Ohio State, or any other university for that matter, and become one.

Now, having said that, I'll be the first to admit, there does seem to be some substance to this old person smell. It can be detected in Granny's room, nursing homes, gerontologist's waiting rooms, churches, and, in some department store restaurants. You can always detect it in the thrift and second-hand shops.

What does it smell like? Well, it's kinda-stale, sorta-medical and sorta-uriney.

What can be done about it? Actually … nothing. Unless, perhaps, one bathes more, stops taking their medications, and/or buys a better grade of adult diapers. Fortunately, for us old-types, we can't smell it.

Which brings me to a topic that is even more concerning: the loss of the sense of smell. *Anosmia* is the dictionary term for those of you who are life-long learners. While it's not as universal as OPS, it affects a significant number of older people. I read once that The National Institutes of Health suggests that most people over the age of 65 experience olfactory deterioration and that it is a *major* problem for people over the age of 80. It should also be noted that aging also affects other senses, hearing, vision, taste (connected to the sense of smell), and touch. (See Memory, Hearing, Vision)

At the outset, it might not seem that losing the sense of smell is a big deal. Except that it can be. Imagine walking past a bakery and not being able to smell the wonderful aroma of baking bread or cookies. As we all know, often, the scent of a familiar aroma from cooking or baking can take us back to our youth. And, anything that can take us back to our youth is a welcome respite from this old business. Even that, however, is something we can live without, if we have to.

But what about when something is burning and we can't smell it? Or, what if food has gone bad? The first thing we usually do is stick the food up to our nose and take a whiff. And what if there's a fire in the basement and we can't smell the smoke? So, even though we can still live without the pleasant smells of food cooking or baking, how do we protect ourselves if we can't smell the bad smells?

Now, I certainly don't want to be the bearer of bad news (seeing as this may very well affect me, too), but I've learned that many serious diseases are associated with olfactory loss or deterioration. The biggest of which is a shorter life span. But I won't go into all of that. But, I do suggest this simple test. From time to time, go into your own closet, a nursing home, or to a second-hand shop and take one deep snort. If none of them smell kinda-stale, sorta-medicinal, or sorta-uriney, it might be time to visit your doctor.

8: Is There a Doctor in the House?

In the world of medicine and health care, opportunities abound for older folks looking for something to do. Doctors love visits from their patients. And hospitals offer private suites for our comfort. Of course, the food leaves something to be desired. It seems more research should be aimed at more palpable food. But, hey, what do we expect for the reasonable price of $999.99/night. And that doesn't even include the cost of aspirin, or the doctor, or tissue. Even so, thanks to modern medicine, people are living longer healthier lives.

But as in all good things, there is a downside—besides vision loss, hearing loss, the loss of smell, dementia … prostate problems.

A mixed blessing, indeed.

It was not too long ago that it was acknowledged that if men lived long enough, most would die *with*, but not *from*, typically slow growing prostate cancer. Today, prostate cancer deaths are on the rise because we are living long enough for it to do us men in. More like a double-edged sword.

Then there's dementia and Alzheimer's. cases seem almost at epidemic levels. Alzheimer's is becoming an increasingly costly health burden. It is almost quaint to remember the elders we knew as kids who were "senile." Of course, it was dementia, and Alzheimer's before we gave it a name. But these were the men and women who were (un)fortunate to live long enough to lapse into that lost and foggy world. There are credible reports in circulation that we are on the verge of a "geriatric tsunami" in that it is not out of reach for Americans to live to be 120.

That world has created another world, the world of the caregiver. We live beyond any reasonable expectation of even half a generation ago. The subplot is that we have to be taken care of. For those who can afford nursing home, assisted living or hospice care, it can provide a reasonably comfortable existence. But affording it is difficult for most. End of life expenses can extend far beyond a reasonable ability to afford it. It can drain a lifetime of savings in months. There is insurance and there is Medicare. Even with that, medical bills can take a financial toll.

I remember reading somewhere that 80 percent of what we spend on health care through our entire lives is spent during our final six months. It is understandably difficult to explain to our kids that this is something to consider saving for. They have enough to save for. There's the mortgage, college debt, unexpected illness and so on.

I'm not even going to get into the Medicaid discussion. It's out there, and it's valuable for those who need and who can take advantage of it. But where Medicaid dollars would send us, is where most of us would not like to go.

There is something else to be thinking about for all parties involved. If it is too expensive to consider nursing homes, assisted living, or even hospice care, the responsibility will likely to fall to a relative. And, to be even more precise, probably to a female relative … usually a daughter.

We men are selfish dolts when it comes to caregiving. We tend to think that job belongs to someone else, and unless we are those in need of the care, we are unlikely to give it much thought. Prolonged illness or incapacity often leads to the caregiver needing care. Their role is exhausting, frustrating and often futile.

There are other considerations that come into play. Depending on the seriousness of the illness, patients and their families are confronted with decisions on hospice care, palliative care, treatment in the home or in an institution. Hospice care is usually a question of providing care and comfort at the end of life. Palliative care is somewhat different and is becoming more widespread. It can be applied to patients who are not terminal, but again, the emphasis is on improving the quality of life and providing comfort during a serious illness. Check your health insurance policy about coverage.

There seems to be growing support for what is called "death with dignity," or "assisted suicide." That's allowing people who choose to depart this world for the next to do so with physician assistance. Needless to say, it is controversial. There are huge ethical considerations for doctors and families. While it is allowed in some states, it is not in most. Those who choose this path, regardless of what the state legally allows or disallows, often turn to a method that is effective though some might call it inhumane or barbaric. These people literally starve themselves to death, refusing nourishment of any kind… food or liquid…until the body shuts down. It usually takes about ten days. We put down our pets more humanely than that.

It is a long and winding road before one gets to that point. As the body wears down with age life can become a series of detours. From the doctor's office, to various medical tests, to surgeries, to rehab. It's expensive and stressful.

More and more Americans are being subjected to an enormous amount of medical testing as they age or become ill. The testing is useful for diagnosing and tracking a multitude of conditions. Testing includes, but is not limited to, analysis of body fluids, imaging, biopsies, and on and on. All are geared to diagnosis and/

or treatment which may or may not involve surgery. The last thing most older people want is surgery. There is a special fear that the older body is too frail to survive time on the operating table. Then there's the rehab which can be taxing in its own right. The alternative, of course, is usually even less appealing.

Awaiting the results of a test can be extraordinarily stressful. There is a tendency to fear and even expect the worst. I have my own story of undergoing a bone scan in connection with a prostate cancer scare. A high PSA count and a biopsy showed a small cancer. But cancer nonetheless. Having lost both parents to the disease this was disturbing news to say the least. If the scan showed that the cancer had spread that would pretty much be the ballgame.

The test was painless. Although as I was undergoing it, monitors were flashing like lights on a pin ball machine. Attendants seemed to be paying a lot of attention to them. Of course, I was convinced that the monitors were proclaiming that I was a doomed man. The tech's reassurances that it was all very normal were not convincing.

My proctologist was a casual acquaintance. How many people can say that? Certainly you'd rather have a "friend" probing where the sun don't shine than someone nursing a grudge. We had mutual friends and would bump into each other occasionally at social events. An appointment was made for us to go over the test results a few days later. To say that those few days were stress free for would be an enormous mischaracterization. Most of the time was spent anticipating bad news and thinking the gravest thoughts, with emphasis on "grave."

The appointment at the doctor's office was set for mid-morning. I arrived a few minutes early and took a seat in the waiting room. The appointment hour came ... and went. Ten minutes. Twenty Minutes. Forty-five minutes. During every second of the prolonged wait, I became more and more convinced that because I and the doctor knew each other socially, the doctor was finding it hard to confront me with the "bad news." It is hard to explain the kind of thoughts I experienced. Emotions ranged from outright fear to various degrees of resignation. I admit those moments waiting were the worst moments of my life. Each tick of the clock convinced me that my personal time was running out.

Turns out the doctor had been delayed by an emergency. The scan proved negative.

The doctor and I discussed options of which there were several, ranging from radiation, surgery, or just letting it go with the understanding of the probability that the slow-growing tumor would not reach the lethal stage for years, if ever during my lifetime. That is a crap shoot I had no difficulty rejecting. Having watched my father lose his cancerous larynx and my mother lose her life to liver cancer, there was no reluctance to tell the doctor to "get that cancerous prostate out of my body."

That was ten years before shortness of breath, and a resulting echocardiogram revealed a 95 percent blockage of the so called "widow maker" artery. There was no time for fear this time. I was on the operating table a few hours later for bypass surgery. A week later, I was home and walking around the block. Modern medicine at work. A generation ago, or perhaps even more recently than that, I would likely have dropped dead with no diagnosis.

So, are medical tests valuable? Are they worth the expense and inconvenience?

What do you think?

9: Scams

If It Sounds Too Good to Be True, It Probably Is

Scammers have been around for generations. Their names have merely changed over the course of time. Flimflam man, snake oil salesman, shark, swindler. However, they are all one in the same. Sonsabitches.

One thing that has added to their game: the Internet. And for a generation that navigates the cyber world with help from their kids and grandkids, if they choose to risk it alone, falling prey to scams is increasingly commonplace. The scams, too, are not limited to the Internet. They can come just as readily by phone, door-to-door, or via televangelists.

So, why is it that, we, as a group, are such frequent and susceptible victims?

Perhaps we are too trusting. Then again, I know many compatriots who don't trust anything or anyone. Yet they can still be, and often are, victims.

Some "credit," if you will, needs to be given to the scammers. They're actually pretty darn good at their chosen career. They know that many older Americans often have acquired some wealth, and have fairly easy access to it either at the bank or under the mattress. Older victims often don't report crimes committed against them. For one thing, they're not sure to whom the crime should be reported. Often the victims do not know for weeks, or even months, that they have been bilked. And when they do realize it, they are embarrassed, so they keep their mouths shut. Or maybe they forget. Sometimes an unfortunate reality (see Memory, Hearing, Eyesight). All in all, scammers have a few things going for them regardless of the sophistication, or lack of it, in their particular operation. Sonsabitches.

We have one neighbor who is still shaking her head over one of the simplest ploys out there. Gypsies. That's what they're called where I live. They are small bands of con artists who travel the country from town to town, find a few marks, then move on to the next town, or county, or state, to work the same con over and over again. They breeze in, and without a "Hi, bye, kiss my—" they disappear without a trace before the authorities even learn of them. Gone. *Poof!* Along with your hard-earned cash. And dignity. Of course, I'd never succumb to such tomfoolery.

And if I did, I sure wouldn't tell you.

Typically, the way they work after having "cased" the neighborhood, is for one of the band to ring the doorbell. Often with a child in tow. When the elderly homeowner responds, the con artist will tell a story of woe and ask to use the phone or for a glass of water. While the owner is preoccupied, an accomplice might enter the home from a rear door looking for anything worth taking. Or the child might wander from one room or another swiping silver candlesticks or anything else that seems of value. Or both could be happening. This is a very basic caper that does not often produce a huge loss. But it's a loss nonetheless. Worst case scenario? The homeowner is subdued, tied up, and put in a closet while the "gypsies" ransack the house or apartment.

There are other scams that can produce a much bigger take. Whoever said there should be laws limiting the sale of guns, has probably never been accosted by one of the principal weapons of a scam artist. The telephone. Of course, a gun would not be of much use in this situation. Unless, of course, you wanted to put the phone out of its misery.

Callers will pretend to represent Medicare or Social Security and pitch much higher benefits. All that's needed is enough personal information to loot a bank account or set up a phony credit card account.

They want cash or access to it in just about every case. But that personal information is golden to the scammer. Obviously, it should not be shared, but sometimes, unfortunately it is. Lowlifes like this prey on the unsuspecting—and oftentimes, trusting—people of our generation who may want nothing more than to talk with someone.

Also, other defrauders play the lottery card. "You've just won the lottery! The only thing you need to do is to send us $50 to get the one million!" (Does the name Bernie Madoff ring a bell?) Some even play on our heartstrings during opportune times: After natural disasters, or during the holidays. Shoot, I've even been hit up for a phony grave plot. But with all of us eventually needing one at some point, I can see where they might get away with this one. You name it, and if there's money to be made, someone, somewhere is out there plotting to relieve you of your hard-earned cash.. These schemers are proficient and smart. They count on a good heart, a bad memory, and even some good "old fashioned" greed.

Even those who promise to save our souls and ease the road to heaven for just a few bucks, mind you, eagerly hold out their hands for a handout. All the while paving the way to their own slice of heaven on earth: in a mansion built on an ocean-side lot in a gated community, surrounded by golf courses, tennis courts, private beaches. Incredibly, tens of thousands of people buy into this hoping to save their souls.

Charlatans, for that's what they are, now have additional opportunities to make a buck. Online. They now have the ability to create authentic looking websites that easily pass for the real enterprise such as a government agency or well-known corporation.

Aside from the famous emails from Nigeria asking for advance money to share lottery winnings, or to help ransom kidnapped schoolgirls, there are any number of email scams trying to get into our wallets and handbags. This is called "phishing." Just like when fishing, the chiseler uses an irresistible bait to snag the unsuspecting and catch vital information. And the cost to send emails by the thousands asking for money for various schemes or for personal information (here we go with that personal information thing again) is minimal at best compared to what the crooks can con out of some. Even if a few people take the bait, they're ahead.

One especially heartbreaking scam involves a little more work, but can be, and has been, effective. Some personal information put online on sites such as Facebook can be of value to scammers. Proud grandparents will often post pictures and information about relatives, often giving the bad guys more than they need to know to set up an effective con.

There have been many occasions in which an unsuspecting grandmother or grandfather gets a panic long distance call from a granddaughter or grandson proclaiming that they have some emergency need for money. Of course, the scammer knows the name of the grandchild and where he or she is located. With that, they're half way home. Even if the voice does not seem quite right, that's easily explained by a bad phone line or cell. "Granny I've had an accident and need five hundred dollars to fix the car." Millions have been swindled in variations of this con.

Another scheme is "vishing." Vishing (voice or VoIP phishing) is an electronic fraud tactic in which individuals are tricked into revealing critical financial or personal information to unauthorized entities. A vishing attack can be conducted by voice email, VoIP (voice over IP), or landline or cellular telephone.

SMiShing (SMS phishing) is a type of phishing attack where mobile phone users receive text messages containing a Web site hyperlink, which, if clicked would download a "Trojan Horse" to the mobile phone yielding personal information. The term SMiShing was coined by David Rayhawk in a McAfee Avert Labs blog on August 25, 2006.

And then there's "pharming.". Pharming is a scamming practice in which malicious code is installed on a personal computer or server, misdirecting users to fraudulent Web sites without their knowledge or consent. Pharming has been called "phishing without a lure."

There is a wonderful bit by radio comedians Bob and Tom about an effective means of dealing with pesky telemarketers, legitimate or otherwise. It goes like this. As soon as you recognize that the telemarketer is someone you don't want to talk to, or don't trust, interrupt their pitch and advise them that you are a homicide detective investigating a murder and that you are at the scene of the crime. Then ask for the caller's personal information. Are they acquainted with the victim? Ask the nature of their business with the victim. Ask for their whereabouts. Advise that the call is being traced as part of the investigation. Suggest that the caller will be called down to the station for questioning. Bob and Tom even asked the caller if he was the victim's gay lover. On and on it went … until finally the caller terminated the call. It actually went on for a lot longer than it would have had I been the caller. I might have been inclined to say, "sorry, I think I have the wrong number." I will suggest, however, that you can just bet that particular telemarketing company pulled that number from its call list. You can find this bit on YouTube.

After all of this phishing, I think I could use a respite and go fishing.

The FBI, like all law enforcement, is concerned about scams perpetrated against the elderly. As noted on the FBI website, senior citizens are especially vulnerable for several reasons: they have accumulated a nest egg, own their home, and have excellent credit. Something con artists look for. So, in order to educate and protect families against fraud, the FBI site includes many of the most common scams that the Bureau encounters. Here's what the Bureau suggests.

Be Proactive: Visit the site and familiarize yourself with everything that these Internet beasts think up to bilk us out of our of our hard-earned cash. Learn what you need to know now!

Don't let your loved ones think you've lost all sense of reasoning or competence. (No need to let them get hold of your money, either!)

One of the most important things to remember: "If it sounds too good to be true, it probably is." So, here is a listing of some no-nonsense things to seriously keep in mind (or at least on the fridge—in case you were to forget).

- *Never sign blank insurance claim forms.*
- *Never give blanket authorization to a medical provider to bill for services rendered.*
- *Ask your medical providers what they will charge and what you will be expected to pay out-of-pocket.*
- *Carefully review your insurer's explanation of the benefits statement. Call your insurer and provider if you have questions.*
- *Do not do business with door-to-door or telephone salespeople who tell you that services of medical equipment are free.*
- *Give your insurance/Medicare identification only to*

those who have provided you with medical services.
- *Keep accurate records of all health care appointments.*
- *Know if your physician ordered equipment for you.*

Fraudulent Medications

One of the things about getting older is that our doctor may order more drugs (or medications, as medical professionals like to call them) to help with things like, oh, blood pressure, peeing—or not. Or peeing when we really don't mean to. At any rate, here are few tidbits for Avoiding Counterfeit Prescription Drugs:

- *Be mindful of appearance. Closely examine the packaging and lot numbers of prescription drugs and be alert to any changes from one prescription to the next. Everyone makes mistakes. Just make sure your meds aren't one of them. Yes, it happens.*

- *Consult your pharmacist or physician if your prescription drug looks different than what you previously received. Or if it looks suspicious. Heaven knows you don't want to receive Viagra for your blood pressure. But wait, maybe you do?*

- *Alert your pharmacist and physician immediately if your medication causes adverse side effects or if your condition does not improve.*

- *Use caution when purchasing drugs on the Internet. Do not purchase medications from unlicensed online distributors or those who sell medications without a prescription. Reputable online pharmacies will have a seal of approval called the Verified Internet Pharmacy Practice Site (VIPPS), provided by the Association of Boards of Pharmacy in the United States.*

- *Be aware that product promotions or cost reductions and other "special deals" may be associated with counterfeit product promotion.*

Funeral and Cemetery Fraud

As if all this information isn't maddening enough, there are also scam artists out there ready to take your nest egg when you die. Funeral and cemetery fraud is a real and growing problem. Here are a few tips for avoiding getting swindled.

- *Be an informed consumer. Take time to call and shop around before making a purchase. Take a friend with you who may offer some perspective to help make difficult decisions. Funeral homes are required to provide detailed general price lists over the telephone or in writing.*
- *Educate yourself fully about caskets before you buy one, and understand that caskets are not required for direct cremations.*
- *Understand the difference between funeral home basic fees for professional services and any fees for additional services.*
- *Know that embalming rules are governed by state*

law and that embalming is not legally required for direct cremations.

- *Carefully read all contracts and purchasing agreements before signing and make certain that all of your requirements have been put in writing.*
- *Make sure you understand all contract cancellation and refund terms, as well as your portability options for transferring your contract to other funeral homes.*
- *Before you consider prepaying, make sure you are well informed. When you do make a plan for yourself, share your specific wishes with those close to you.*
- *As a general rule governing all of your interactions as a consumer, do not allow yourself to be pressured into making purchases, signing contracts, or committing funds. These decisions are yours and yours alone.*

Fraudulent "Anti-Aging" Products

Again, if it sounds too good to be true, it probably is. None of us want to get old—or look old—before our time. But we all age, and scammers prey on this and are ready to sell us on the latest "secret formula" or "anti-aging breakthrough". Don't fall for it. Always be ready to ask questions and do some research.

- *Don't be afraid to ask questions about the product. Find out exactly what it should and should not do for you.*
- *Research a product thoroughly before buying it. Call*

the Better Business Bureau to find out if other people have complained about the product.

- *Be wary of products that claim to cure a wide variety of illnesses—particularly serious ones—that don't appear to be related.*
- *Be aware that testimonials and/or celebrity endorsements are often misleading.*
- *Be very careful of products that are marketed as having no side effects.*
- *Question products that are advertised as making visits to a physician unnecessary.*
- *Always consult your doctor before taking any dietary or nutritional supplement.*

Telemarketing Fraud

If you are age 60 or older—and especially if you are an older woman living alone—you may be a special target of people who sell bogus products and services by telephone. Telemarketing scams often involve offers of free prizes, low-cost vitamins and health care products, and inexpensive vacations.

There are warning signs to these scams. If you hear these—or similar—"lines" from a telephone salesperson, just say "no thank you," and hang up the telephone:

- *"You must act now, or the offer won't be good."*
- *"You've won a free gift, vacation, or prize." But you have to pay for "postage and handling" or other*

charges.

- *"You must send money, give a credit card or bank account number, or have a check picked up by courier."* You may hear this before you have had a chance to consider the offer carefully.
- *"You don't need to check out the company with anyone."* The callers say you do not need to speak to anyone, including your family, lawyer, accountant, local Better Business Bureau, or consumer protection agency.
- *"You don't need any written information about the company or its references."*
- *"You can't afford to miss this high-profit, no-risk offer."*

Tips for Avoiding Telemarketing Fraud:

- *It's very difficult to get your money back if you've been cheated over the telephone. Before you buy anything by telephone, remember:*
- *Don't buy from an unfamiliar company. Legitimate businesses understand that you want more information about their company and are happy to comply.*
- *Always ask for and wait until you receive written material about any offer or charity. If you get brochures about costly investments, ask someone whose financial advice you trust to review them. But, unfortunately, beware—not everything written down is true.*

- *Always check out unfamiliar companies with your local consumer protection agency, Better Business Bureau, state attorney general, the National Fraud Information Center, or other watchdog groups. Unfortunately, not all bad businesses can be identified through these organizations.*
- *Obtain a salesperson's name, business identity, telephone number, street address, mailing address, and business license number before you transact business. Some con artists give out false names, telephone numbers, addresses, and business license numbers. Verify the accuracy of these items.*
- *Before you give money to a charity or make an investment, find out what percentage of the money is paid in commissions and what percentage actually goes to the charity or investment.*
- *Before you send money, ask yourself a simple question. "What guarantee do I really have that this solicitor will use my money in the manner we agreed upon?"*
- *Don't pay in advance for services. Pay for services only after they are delivered.*
- *Be wary of companies that want to send a messenger to your home to pick up money, claiming it is part of their service to you. In reality, they are taking your money without leaving any trace of who they are or where they can be reached.*
- *Always take your time making a decision. Legitimate*

companies won't pressure you to make a snap decision.

- *Don't pay for a "free prize." If a caller tells you the payment is for taxes, he or she is violating federal law.*
- *Before you receive your next sales pitch, decide what your limits are—the kinds of financial information you will and won't give out on the telephone.*
- *Be sure to talk over big investments offered by telephone salespeople with a trusted friend, family member, or financial advisor. It's never rude to wait and think about an offer.*
- *Never respond to an offer you don't understand thoroughly.*
- *Never send money or give out personal information such as credit card numbers and expiration dates, bank account numbers, dates of birth, or social security numbers to unfamiliar companies or unknown persons.*
- *Be aware that your personal information is often brokered to telemarketers through third parties.*
- *If you have been victimized once, be wary of persons who call offering to help you recover your losses for a fee paid in advance.*
- *If you have information about a fraud, report it to state, local, or federal law enforcement agencies.*

Internet Fraud

As web use among senior citizens increases, so do their chances to fall victim to Internet fraud. Internet Fraud includes non-delivery of items ordered online and credit and debit card scams. Please visit the FBI's Internet Fraud webpage for details about these crimes and tips for protecting yourself from them.

Investment Schemes

As they plan for retirement, senior citizens may fall victim to investment schemes. These may include advance fee schemes, prime bank note schemes, pyramid schemes, and Nigerian letter fraud schemes. Please visit the Common Fraud Schemes webpage for more information about these crimes and tips for protecting yourself from them.

Reverse Mortgage Scams

The FBI and the U.S. Department of Housing and Urban Development Office of Inspector General (HUD-OIG) urge consumers, especially senior citizens, to be vigilant when seeking reverse mortgage products. Reverse mortgages, also known as home equity conversion mortgages (HECM), have increased more than 1,300 percent between 1999 and 2008, creating significant opportunities for fraud perpetrators.

Reverse mortgage scams are engineered by unscrupulous professionals in a multitude of real estate, financial services, and related companies to steal the equity from the property of unsuspecting senior citizens or to use these seniors to unwittingly aid the fraudsters in stealing equity from a flipped property.

In many of the reported scams, victim seniors are offered free homes, investment opportunities, and foreclosure or refinance assistance. They are also used as straw buyers in property flipping scams. Seniors are frequently targeted through local churches and investment seminars, as well as television, radio, billboard, and mailer advertisements.

A legitimate HECM loan product is insured by the Federal Housing Authority. It enables eligible homeowners to access the equity in their homes by providing funds without incurring a monthly payment. Eligible borrowers must be 62 years or older who occupy their property as their primary residence and who own their property or have a small mortgage balance. See the FBI/HUD Intelligence Bulletin for specific details on HECMs as well as other foreclosure rescue and investment schemes.

Tips for Avoiding Reverse Mortgage Scams:

- *Do not respond to unsolicited advertisements.*
- *Be suspicious of anyone claiming that you can own a home with no down payment.*
- *Do not sign anything that you do not fully understand.*
- *Do not accept payment from individuals for a home you did not purchase.*
- *Seek out your own reverse mortgage counselor.*
- *If you are a victim of this type of fraud and want to file a complaint, submit information through your local FBI office. You may also file a complaint with HUD-*

*OIG at www.hud.gov/complaints/fraud_waste.cfm
or by calling HUD's hotline at 1-800-347-3735.*

Here's one that is not on the FBI list. It's not even a scam, but you'd better get involved in this one with your eyes wide open, and at your own risk and. It's the extended care pitch from a friendly insurance agent, or financial adviser, all of whom can be seen licking their chops over the prospect of a healthy commission. There's nothing inherently wrong with commissions. But you need to be confident your interest is being represented first and foremost.

The sales tactics are not scare tactics, unless you're afraid of a lifetime of savings being wiped out, or unless you fear having to rely on Medicaid finding a bed for you in what will likely be a second or third or fourth rate place. You may be afraid that your kids or other loved ones could have their life savings wiped out attending to your needs, leaving them with little or nothing when they get old and reach the extended care age. It is these fears that can be preyed upon.

It must be emphasized that this is an important decision and should be given a lot of thought with advice from someone who is competent to advise, preferably one in whom you are confident your interest trumps a possible commission. If it's what you need and want, he or she has rightfully earned that commission. Remember, there is a lot of fine print in these policies. You might want to think about an attorney to interpret. Here are a few key things to keep in mind.

- *To begin with, extended care insurance is expensive. More so the longer you wait to sign on the dotted line. It can run into several thousand dollars a year.*

- *The policies typically don't apply to the first three months of a stay. Three months is about the length of the average stay. That's why insurance companies compile actuarial data.*

- *A typical payout for lower range premiums is $150 dollars a day (after three months) and policies normally provide coverage for three years. That's a little over $164,000. You should calculate whether you have savings to cover that range and decide whether you want to.*

- *The insurance companies usually have a long list of requirements to be met for the extended care payout. Often, unless you have been "doctor certified" to have hands on, or other specified assistance needs, they can refuse to pay. For instance, if you can give yourself a bath, dress yourself, or eat on your own, you might not qualify while assuming you are qualified.*

- *With 70 million baby boomers now into their senior years, will insurers have the resources to pay at all if a large number of boomers carry the extended care insurance?*

- *And, this note. The Wall Street Journal reports that only 4 percent of American seniors currently reside in nursing homes. You may never have the need.*

There is no denying there is an entirely different equation when it comes to long term illnesses such as Alzheimer's. That can range over several years and represent a big expense. A BIG expense. Long term care for Alzheimer's patients can easily run to about $100,000 a year.

As mentioned earlier, this requires a lot of thought and advice from family, and competent, trusted, people who have nothing to gain no matter what you decide. It can be overwhelming.

Convincing arguments can be made for self-insuring. That is making some basic calculations to determine if savings can cover the averages. Among the calculations: would you rather use those savings on yourself, or are you more interested in leaving the money you worked all your life to accumulate to children?

Does anyone have the number of the Hemlock Society?

10: Bucket List

When is it too late for a bucket list?

After you've kicked the bucket.

Why is it that so many of us fail to do or accomplish the things we've always wanted to do or accomplish? Or, if we do consider them, we decide against taking action because we think, "We're too old!" It's a well-known fact that if someone thinks they can't do something, it's more than likely they can't. Same thing if we think we are too old to do something. And, it's been my observation in recent decades, that if that's the way you feel, odds are against your getting much older.

There is a growing movement across the country today: "Before I Die Festivals." that seems to be gaining some traction. Not only does the discussion revolve around medical care and end-of-life issues with some festivals offering presentations by funeral directors, talk of crema- tion versus traditional burial, participation even includes

visiting cemeteries. It's a group approach to bucket listing in which participants gather to discuss the kind of
things they want to realize or accomplish before they
die. It all begins with participants discussing death itself.

I recently listened to a report on NPR by researchers
Becca Levy, a professor of epidemiology and psychology
at the Yale School of Public Health, and Patricia Boyle,
a neuropsychologist and behavioral scientist at Rush
Alzheimer's Disease Center in Chicago.

In one study, Levy looked at people's attitudes about
aging as they aged, looking at them first when they were
in late middle age and then following them over time.
She found that "Some of these people thought of older
people as weak or dependent. Others thought of them as
experienced or wise. What she found was that the people
who had a positive view of aging lived about seven-and-
a-half years longer than the people who saw aging in a
negative light." Plus, in another study, she found "that
middle-aged people who had no cognitive impairment but
did have negative views of aging were more likely to later
develop the brain changes associated with Alzheimer's
disease. Still another showed that "the more negative their
views, the worse those brain changes were." But one study
did show that a positive attitude in older adults assisted in
recovery from major health issues."

According to researcher Patricia Boyle, "Having
something that gives one's life a sense of purpose can pay

amazing health dividends." And she notes, "It doesn't have to be something complicated and lofty, just something that's goal oriented and gives you a sense of accomplishment." She says, "People who have the sense that their life is meaningful are much less likely to suffer early mortality, [and] they're less like to develop disability; that is, trouble taking care of themselves." Additional benefits include "they're less likely to suffer strokes … and develop Alzheimer's disease, and they have much less cognitive decline." And the research of both Levy and Boyle, suggests that if people don't assume that they'll be useless when they're older, the payoff could be huge." (You can listen to the interview here: https://www.npr.org/sections/health-shots/2016/05/28/479751942/could-thinking-positively-about-aging-be-the-secret-of-health)

So remember, as long as you're still breathing,
you still have time.

So back to that bucket list. What can we all do to latch onto those additional seven and a half years and create meaning in our lives? Travel, visit grandkids, play golf, garden, volunteer, and read. That friend I mentioned earlier who had done everything on his bucket list and found himself bored and no longer fulfilled? He went to work as a greeter at Walmart. He's apparently as happy as he was when touring the Greek islands, largely because he was once again doing what he had done for decades in business: interact with people. In other words, not only did he have someplace to go every day, his life again had meaning, purpose. So, it looks like waking up with no purpose is a short drive to not waking up at all. Or, not wanting to. I'm not quite ready to do that yet. What about you?

Other ways to keep purpose in our lives is to stay socially active—maintain old friendships (at least the ones that don't drag you down), make new ones, and get together frequently. Interaction with others keeps the brain active. Don't just sit around and binge watch Netflix or Amazon Prime. Sure, we all need downtime … just not all of the time.

Of course, there are other ways to give meaning to our lives (young or old): start a new hobby, learn to play the piano, or violin. Why not a banjo or horn or tuba? And practice at the kids' houses. Payback. And what better way to tax your brain than to learn a new language? Or learn to play chess? Even if you play like I do, the brain cells and concentration it takes to decipher moves is much better than sitting and staring at a TV. Besides, at this point in our lives, we have much more time to practice and have the time to do whatever we want. Hey, you Millennials, don't be jealous! You will be stepping into our shoes sooner than you realize.

And you know what? Who says you have to retire? What better way to remain active and keep the old brain cells recharged?

Sure, no matter if you retire or not, some things you want to do may seem out of sequence—the timing is wrong. Who wrote the rules that we're supposed to learn to play the piano as kids? Does that mean we shouldn't or couldn't or wouldn't want to learn something new at the ripe old age of eighty? Nope. Don't let anyone tell you your advanced age is an impediment to learning or accomplishment. Sure, our bucket lists may have to be tweaked along the way, but hey, that's part of the fun and privilege of getting old. And as long as our ticker is tick-tocking, it's not too late to do anything. Unless of course, it is.

So, when is too late? There is always time … until there is no time. Time, for the most part, is relative and need not be determined by the ticking of a clock.

Which prompts me to think about Christmas. (Just go with it.) In May 1942, Bing Crosby recorded *White Christmas*, written by Irving Berlin. Also, *The Christmas Song (Chestnuts Roasting on an Open Fire)* was written by Mel Tormé and Bob Wells during a July California heat wave. Their idea was that if they wrote about something cold, it would give them some relief from the oppressive heat. Thinking about Jack Frost nipping at your nose must have been very refreshing in 100-degree heat. Incidentally, a bit of trivia (which also keeps the old brains cells plugging along): Irving Berlin and Mel Tormé were Jewish. Not an important fact in and of itself, other than to note that not too many Gentiles are known for writing popular and timeless songs about Passover, Rosh Hashana, or Yom Kippur.

11: Mortality

Be sure to attend the funerals of your friends,
or else they won't go to yours. —Yogi Berra

At some point, as the sands of time slip through that old hourglass, we do think about mortality, and there's no place where we confront the subject more directly than when we read the obit page in our local newspaper. It is a daily reminder that one day our own picture and life history in one hundred words or less will be there for someone else to read.

Me? I don't check the obits anymore. I'm afraid I'll find my name. (Old Joke)

For many contemporaries (at least in my age group), it is one of the first, if not the first page they read in the daily newspaper, either online or the rather shrinking inked pages. Ironically, many newspapers are on financial life support, and some are finding their own names in the obits.

Who among us has not turned to the page to learn that someone we know, or once knew, has gone on to the great reward? It is a chillingly, uncomfortable experience to personalize mortality. We want to know the circumstances of death. Was it illness? Was it an accident? Was it the dreaded, "died of natural causes?" This is just another way of saying that old bodies sooner or later just give up the ghost and lose the ability to hang in there.

Even more unsettling is seeing the ages of the departed. For some reason, I find myself automatically calculating their age compared to mine. *Wow. She was five years younger than I am now. He was just a year older than I am. Will I be next?*

Few of us, however, are willing to accept that we may be next in line. We are geared to anticipate extended longevity. We are geared to fight for our lives. To not give up. Many of us—if not all of us—gear ourselves to mentally compare our lifespan with that of the ninety-five-year-old person who smoked and drank every day. Bad habits be damned! And therein lies the hope that all our bad habits, too, will be overridden. Of course, for some of us, they won't be. But I'll think about that tomorrow. Maybe....

Acknowledging our own mortality is a gradual thing. At age fifteen or twenty, we don't even think about it. For many, we have not yet been touched by death. I was eighteen when my mother died at age fifty-three and I still, even then, didn't consider my own mortality. At eighteen, we consider ourselves invincible, indestructible.

Immortal. That's why the twenty-somethings' make such good fighter pilots and entrepreneurs. Nothing can bring them down. Until, of course it does. But again, our universal, built-in defense mechanism kicks in. "That won't happen to me." Even now, at my young, old age, I have a tendency to ignore the facts. I still bury this mortality card somewhere deep in the deck. Fantasy does, after all, have its merits!

When my mother died, I was, of course, heartbroken, but never reckoned I would not go on to live a long, long time. After all, I was a kid and fifty-three seemed a long way off. My reality check came when I reached fifty-three. It was then I began to wonder, not only whether I would survive my fifty-third year, but what would happen if my life just stopped, as hers had at that same age? I must admit, I was not thinking of the impact of my demise on family, friends, career, and plans. I was thinking of the impact on me!

Now that I have lived twenty-five years longer than my mother, and ten years longer than my father, any sense of immortality has long ago disappeared. Not only does reading the obit page, and checking off each lost friend, relative, or acquaintance, and noting their age compared to my own, see to that, so, too, have two major surgeries. And, any notion of "It can't happen to me," flew the coop long ago.

Still, waking up in the morning for a lot more mornings gets my vote. However, if kicking the bucket has to happen at all—and the actuarial tables are quite consistent that all of us will die at some point—dying in one's sleep does have some appeal.

There is, though, also an intriguing appeal to the thought of death. Some believe in life after death, and even if you don't, contemplating eternal life is, after all, comforting. We've all heard those tales of out-of-body and near-death experiences. They're the ones about that moment of death when the dying are drawn toward an appealing light, and there in the distance, relatives and loved ones beckon.

The problem with that, though, is that there are few people who have the capacity to tell the story. There are similar stories, too, told by people who have been clinically dead on the operating table, or at the scene of an accident, but who survived. They tell of floating over the operating table or accident scene, and see themselves, including their own death. Something else I've heard all my life is that at the time of death, our lives flash before our eyes. One thing I do know is that if no one who has actually died never gets to tell us if it's true, I'd certainly be happy to be the first!

As I've grown older, I often have middle-of-the-night flashbacks—isolated, random recollections of when I was very young. I've revisited people, places, and things I have not thought about in years—even actually forgotten about—which is really rather eerie. Interestingly, too, I am a spectator rather than a participant. It's as if I were watching a movie with random moments of my life And now, such moments happen with increasing frequency. Who knows, maybe the filing cabinet in my head, like a computer that has only so much memory, is overloaded and needs to purge itself. Defragment, so to speak, in order for our brains to operate more efficiently, and we are privy to the process. Still, it's a bit disconcerting. I just sure hope this isn't what they mean about your life flashing before your eyes!

Baseball great Yogi Berra was quite philosophical about death … as referenced at the beginning of this chapter. *Be sure to attend the funerals of your friends, or else they won't go to yours.* He also had this memorable line when his wife asked him where he wanted to be buried. His answer: "I don't know. Surprise me."

Surprises are the last thing you want to spring on your family. So how to prevent this? Pre-plan. Yes, it's still hard to think of our own demise, but when our loved ones do have to face our death, pre-planning our own funeral arrangements will make it a bit easier on them. Besides, think of it in positive terms: you get to pick out your final resting place, decide the music, readings, who you do (and definitely don't) want to say a few words about how remarkable you were!

Pre-planning doesn't just mean planning your funeral. Here are a few other realities to keep in mind as you plan for that day.

Health care directives, also called living wills, are another highly important consideration, and for many, are difficult to think about. These directives can include everything from organ donation to your wishes concerning life support. Tough to think about, but we all should so our loved ones—or worse, yet, strangers—have to make the decisions for us.

For example, if you do not wish to be kept alive artificially when there is no hope of survival, this should be noted in the directive with the designation of a power of attorney. The power of attorney is given to an individual you appoint to make your health decisions for you if you are no longer able to do so. You probably would prefer to choose someone who does not owe you money.

Other issues concern guardianship and conservatorship. These are appointees who are designated to handle affairs when the designator is deemed incompetent to make critical decisions. Decisions can range from medications to payment of bills.

This is becoming an increasing issue as people live longer, and the number of cases of dementia and Alzheimer's increase. The appointed guardian would make these decisions. A conservator should be designated to handle financial decisions.

A couple of more serious notes: Make sure your last will and testament is up to date. (Or better yet, establish a living trust. See below). Otherwise, your loved ones will need to go through probate to settle your estate if proper preparations have not been made—and you don't want that. Why? Lawyers, Uncle Sam, the state you live in. They'll all take their piece of your pie *before* your loved ones get one dollar, if there's any left after the others get through.

Estate planning can give you control over who gets what, assuring that most of what you want to happen, will. The last thing any of us would want is to have relatives squabbling over the assets—and, sadly, many times that's exactly what happens without a plan. There's an upside to this, though. Even though you won't be around to revel in it, you have the chance to have the last laugh, and when appropriate, "get even."

One thing to note here, a simple will may not be enough to resolve all of your final wishes or intentions. Yes, it is better than nothing and everyone—even the young—need one. Some, however, due to the number of assets, may need to set up a trust. Gathering all your assets in your estate into a trust will keep everything within the trust out of court.

Trusts are a bit more complicated than a simple will. You'll definitely need to choose a trustee or trustees and executors who will be dedicated to fulfilling your wishes, and who will be deemed fair by your heirs. You know who they are, and who they are not.

My estate planner tells the story of a nasty family

dispute that went to court and cost thousands of dollars to litigate. The fight was over a lamp! So, it's not a bad idea to talk with family when planning one's estate to determine who wants what. This may be awkward for kids, and you, but this enables things to be set right with the world. Besides, if there is a potential fight between siblings or relatives over something while you are still here, you have the option of getting rid of the damn thing!

Another element of planning that some consider anxiety provoking is planning for the final disposition of one's remains. The last thing most rational people feel comfortable with is envisioning their own lifeless body and its disposal. But as we all know, we can't just let our loved ones sit us up in a chair by the fireplace and stay there forever. I don't think we need to go into why.

The big question is *how* do you want *you* to be disposed of? The easy answer? What difference does it make? In reality, however, the answer comes down to burial or cremation. And, they are not mutually exclusive.

The traditional funeral in this country usually involves an undertaker, a funeral home, and an open or closed casket. Keep mine closed, please. I can't abide the thought that people will file by saying or thinking, "he never looked better."

Cremation is seemingly becoming more and more popular. Practitioners are even advertising on television. Some people blanch at the thought of it. Though it is efficient, environmentally friendly, and a choice that is a lot easier for claustrophobics who cannot stand the thought of spending eternity (afterlife or no) cooped up in a box and buried six feet under. And now there's an even more environmentally friendly option on the horizon: alkaline hydrolysis, also called also called biocremation, resomation, flameless cremation, or water cremation. Without going into the details, you basically come out the other end of the process in a slurry of harmless liquid and an urn full of biodegradable bone and minerals. (You can learn more here: https://www.nytimes.com/2017/10/19/business/flameless-cremation.html)

With flames or without, there's still the question of what to do with what's left over. Some may want their ashes scattered. Planning ahead gives you the option to choose where you want your remains deposited and to share that information with the kiddos. Maybe even plan a family outing around this?

Others may decide to give a share of themselves to the kids. For me, this is a bit creepy. If someone's ashes were offered to me, I'd give a big, "No thanks!" Even if it were Mom, Dad, or Granny. I have heard of one man who designated that some of his ashes be included in a ring, to be worn evermore by his partner. Although, I'd pass on this, too, the partner readily accepted the idea and gives reverential status to the token.

Believe it or not, it is even possible to make diamonds from human ashes. I kid you not. I can hear the conversation now:

"Hey there, nice ring!"

"Thanks. It's dad."

Conversely, there are those who prefer that to an eternity of repose in an urn on someone's mantle, or in a garage, or even buried in a mausoleum or in the ground with a headstone. Care should be considered, however, if the urn is placed on the mantle, coffee table, or shelf. The family cat, or an overzealous housekeeper, could possibly knock it over. Then how would you clean that up? Vacuum cleaner? Dustpan? Wet sponge? Speaking of cats, why were many of Egypt's ancients laid to rest with their cats? What's that all about?

Some have even requested their ashes be mixed with masonry, garden soil, and even food. Food? As Hannibal Lector might have said, "We're having Grandma for dinner tonight."

"Thanks. I'll just go out and grab a Big Mac."

Another item that should be on your to-do list is to make sure your insurance beneficiaries are current. There are times when someone you have listed may have died before you. Along with that, whoever is the executor of your will, should be made aware of how many policies you have, as well as where they are kept. You don't want them fishing through everything to find them.

A surprise to many survivors when tying up loose ends is the death certificate. Actually, your executors will need several death certificates. One for every transaction related to your death, such as insurance, social security, taxes, among others. Recently, I came across an article on www.thebalance.com, entitled, "Important Papers to Locate When Someone Dies." There is a detailed listing of everything your executor will need to settle your estate—everything from pre-nuptial agreements, to business documents, to utility bills and bank accounts, etc.

12: We Are Our Parents

Never say never. Because chances are you'll have to eat those words. Granted, there are myriad books on the market today that assist first-time parents with the ins and outs of raising a child. But more times than not, after another kiddo comes along, that book has found its way to the trash bin or the second-hand store.

And then it happens. The sudden realization that you just did exactly what your parents did to you. Admit it. You might as well, because you know it's true. Actually, as we were parented is the only real template for parenting. For better or worse. And, of course, it's the only template our parents had. God only knows how many past generations influenced our own parenting techniques.

And just like our parents and their parents before them, there are certain truisms that come with the entire parenting process. Parents will invariably disagree with the kind of music their kids listen to, the way they spend their time, their study habits, often the friends they keep, the kind of clothes they wear, hair styles and anything else that reeks of something different than what they experienced in their teenage years. Today's young people disagree with their parents just as those parents disagreed with theirs. Take tattoos, for instance. A no-no in the minds of most parents back in the day. Tattoos were more or less limited to members of the military. It was fairly common during World War II, Korea, and Vietnam. Then they were put on the no shelf ... until recently. In case you haven't noticed, they're back!

I remember very distinctly my father wondering what kind of music I was listening to when I was playing Roy Hamilton's "Ebb Tide" on my 45 RPM record player. His words went something like this: "Is that what they're calling music these days?" He grew up in the Rudy Vallee era, to which I might have said, "Is that what they called music in your day?" Needless to say, Hamilton and Vallee are absolutely benign compared to what today's teens enjoy. (I think I just helped make my own point.)

My own contribution to the continuum was questioning my son's fondness for the Grateful Dead. There was one occasion in which I was driving him and a friend someplace, a ballgame or such. I was playing "oldies," which, in this case, means a selection of music from the fifties. The kids laughed at the music. I did not take it well. "I'll have you know," I said with indignation, "that this music is the ancestor of your own 'crap' they call music these days." While they laughed, I had the unspoken pleasure (or perhaps it was spoken) of knowing that one day those two kids would have a similar conversation with their children.

By the way, my daughter has always enjoyed show tunes. She knows a lot more about the work of Rogers and Hammerstein and Stephen Sondheim than I do about Lady Gaga and Jay-Z. A chip off the old block, she is, and therefore my enlightened one. But she still sports a tattoo. It's in a fairly private location. I have no idea what kind (of tattoo) it is. I don't know if she won't show me what it is, because of where it is, or because of what it is.

I have no grandchildren. I am impressed with those contemporaries who do and with the way it has changed them. It's an absolute metamorphosis. I think back on the way they acted as young parents. Hassled much of the time. Spending hour upon hour chauffeuring kids to ballgames when the adults would rather have been doing something else, like golf or shopping, perhaps sleeping. After the kids left home (some maybe for the third or fourth time), parents found relief in their empty nest. Time to do the things they'd had on their bucket list. Time to do what they wanted on their own terms. And then it happens.

Grandkids.

The bucket list hits the trash. Their language takes a deep dive. No more complete sentences. "Goo goo" and Ga ga" and all kinds of unnatural gurgling noises erupt spontaneously.

Now their world revolves around that little bitty person who will carry on their genes. Every waking moment is consumed by that next-generation bundle of joy. They profess to love it, and they must, because it seems that all their decisions revolve around being close to, and having frequent access to, the chubby cherubs. It is imperative they live within striking distance, whether by foot, bike, or car. Or, when necessary, close to an airport.

I do want to confess at this stage of the game, to being from the W.C. Fields school of relating to kids that belong to other people. For instance, "Anyone who hates children and animals can't be all bad." Or, "I like children if they're properly cooked." Don't hate me. Not having grandchildren, I'm speaking in ignorance. But when and if the next generation comes along in our family, then my manner of speaking may likely also take a turn to the south.

But don't count on it.

As I see it, just as parents think they know better than their kids. Grandparents will think they still know more than their kids, even though they are adults and parents themselves. Their grandkids will not be exposed to the right food, the right clothes, how their room is decorated, the right lullaby, the right nap schedule, the right formula, the right 'anything.'

And now, not only do the new parents have one set of grandparents advising them, there are two, each with its own notion of what is right for baby. This will inevitably result in tension and wear and tear in the relationship between the grandparents and the monsters attempting to raise their precious grandchildren.

Discord with a capital 'D'.

Remember that "template? We have a total of six adults, two sets of grandparents, and the actual parents, all with various experiences as children and parents, and with all trying to have some measure of influence over every facet of how baby's upbringing is handled. Along with this, thanks to DNA, influences carried forward from generations past are brought into the equation.

All of this adds up to an emotional stew, which, while simmering, may very well cause Mama and Daddy, both sets of grandparents, and the baby as well, to wail inconsolably.

Of course, it'll be Mama and Daddy who will be awake at 3:00 a.m., changing poopy diapers—after the sweet pea has thrown up down daddy's bare back—all the while pacing the floor begging the baby to stop crying, please. *Please!*

All the while, Gramps and Gram will be tucked tightly in their bed dreaming of their new little angel.

Add to all this the pressure of choosing the baby's name. It's almost too much to think about.

Then there's religion. Gadzooks ... let's not even go there. Makes me want to cry.

13: Computers & Cell Phones & Facebook, Oh My!

Computers. Smart Phones. Facebook. Twitter. Instagram.

On to the next chapter! Not really.

Fact is, I do use Facebook and Twitter. I send an occasional text, too. I have a Smart Phone, which my Millennial daughter helped me buy and taught me how to use. I purchased the phone for emergencies. So far it's worked. I have had no emergencies. I also understand I have GPS which can help me if I get lost. That's worked, too. I have never been lost. All in all, though, I'm not quite sure how the GPS works.

Technology is a big part of my work, and a necessary part. Yes, I do scratch my head a lot. Not because of its complexity (technology not my head). Rather, because of much of the content. Not mine, of course. My content is just fine and dandy. What baffles me, is how and why so many people think that so many other people care about what they are doing at any given moment. Do we really need to know that one friend is having a beer at the ballgame or that they are walking the dog in the park? And do we really need a picture of said event to prove it?

What is technology doing to real conversation? Conversations are becoming a lost art. I've seen groups of young people sitting at the same table, or in the same room, texting a friend who is sitting across from them, emailing rather than picking up the phone to say hello, or sharing what's going on in their life via Facebook, rather than sending an old-fashioned letter, or engaging with each other face to face.

Plus, I see so many doing something I cannot master. Banging out a text or email with their thumbs on a tiny keypad with the kind of speed I can barely achieve on a normal keyboard. This is the kind of talent that is completely contrary to the old adage, "all thumbs." I can't do it without having to correct every other character.

I do know that many older people shy away from the new technology, be it cell phones, computer, or social media. I'm not sure why. Perhaps it's just that all of it is new and not easily understood. Perhaps it's arthritic hands and fingers. Maybe it's the jargon that scares them: wifi, bandwidth, spam, apps, and now the completely new definition of cookies. Maybe it's because technology changes with a pace that makes planned obsolescence seem quaint. At one time, people kept a car three years or longer. Now, your smart phone is all but obsolete overnight.

For years, my wife would no more think of touching my computer, much less actually use it, than I would think of throwing out her shoes and purses. She was absolutely convinced that if she did something wrong she would erase everything on the device. Little did she know that that might not be such bad idea. My concern, had I thought she might ever take the old Dell for a test drive, was not that she would accidentally erase anything, but rather she might find some of the things I have "tucked" away in some obscure folder.

While the technology does seem to intimidate many older people, there are some that embrace that change. Not because it has become such an important and omni-present force in today's world, as it has, but rather it's the grandchildren! Once, for lots of grandparents that didn't live in close proximity to the grandchildren, they might see them once, twice a year. Now, however, they can now bring the grandkids into their lives every day. Contact is available 24/7 through email, texting, Skype, Twitter, you name it. Pictures, too, can be had on a moment's notice, tracking every drop of spittle, every lost tooth, every prom and graduation, from kindergarten to college. All the at the mere flick of an arthritic finger.

For some of us, this has the additional advantage of fewer in-person visits, along with fewer visits to distant parts of the country, or other parts of the world. Fewer occasions of little ones breaking things when they come to call, or of throwing up on that favorite comforter. Now we can watch them do those things in their own homes.

This new and exciting technology adds a twist to the little ones' visits. You no longer have to wave goodbye and feign regret when the visit is over. You simply hit the 'Off' button. *Poof!* They're gone.

14: Fly the Coop or Turn Up the Heat

Why are so many of us drawn to places like Florida and Arizona during the winter months and become snowbirds? One simple reason. We are cold!

As a youngster, I used to dread having to visit older relatives. It wasn't that I didn't love them and the treats they always had for me and the other kids. I wasn't too crazy about Tomato Aspic or Cream of Celery soup for lunch, but there were always cookies, too. They were often Hydrox rather than Oreo or something homemade, but hey, a cookie was a cookie back then.

The thing that really bothered me was the heat. Invariably, their homes, apartments, or assisted living rooms were nudging thermostats toward Death Valley norms, no matter what the season. The central air (if it was even on) would push tropical breezes throughout their homes, ensuring longevity to any self-respecting palm or eucalyptus tree.

While my T-shirt would begin sticking to my sweaty chest within moments of arrival, the featured hosts would sit un-perspired in a heavy sweater, often with a hefty comforter wrapped snuggly around their legs. A shawl was often draped around the shoulders or at the ready to be whisked into service the moment the heat pump failed.

The memory of it all is still very vivid. Especially as I sit here writing ... dressed in comfy sweats, heavy socks, and fuzzy slippers, wondering if it really is ninety-two degrees outside. And, if it is, why am I so uncomfortably cool. No, let me correct that. Cold! *I'm cold!* Even with the thermostat set at a balmy 75 degrees, the flow of air chills me to the bone.

Now, I do not live alone. Temperature disputes are a source of some ongoing friction with my wife who is ten years younger and who is perspiring heavily as she bustles around the house. Her time will come. Somewhere, a wool comforter is lurking.

How many times have I wished that the heating and cooling system at our place was as effective at keeping me warm in the winter as it is cooling me to excess in the summer? I suppose it stands to reason that if a room temperature of 75 degrees keeps me uncomfortably cool in the summer, it would not warm me up at 75 in the winter.

The obvious questions in all this is why does cold affect old people so much of the time, especially their hands and feet? Well, the most obvious answer? Because they are old.

There can be other things that come into play, too, but first and foremost, it's because we are old. So, what is happening?

Old age. Wait, I already said that.

When a woman experiences the hot flashes of menopause, it is actually an issue of thermoregulation. So is feeling cold just a few short years later.

Our bodies change with age. Our hair thins. Faces and guts sag. Even our skin gets thinner. There is some evidence a reduction in the fat layer below the skin, which helps the body retain heat, may be a culprit for the coldness older people feel.

How about thin blood? I have theorized, probably erroneously, that I get cold in a warm place because I'm on a blood thinner. I will grab at any theory that replaces the "getting older" one, even though I've been making excuses for all sorts of things I know nothing about. We—the old *and* the young—can rationalize anything.

Medications and medical conditions can also have an impact. Cardiovascular problems can be an issue, as can diabetes. Medications that slow the heart rate can affect the extremities, which means cold hands or feet. Blood flow is a key factor to being alive (or being dead for that matter), and any medication that changes that flow has an impact.

There seems to be a medical consensus that, more often than not, it's a consequence of our metabolism slowing down. Everything else is slowing down, why should metabolism be any different? And some things have not only ALREADY slowed down, they've come to a complete, absolute, dead stop. This, of course, has a compound effect on the body's ability to maintain the normal body temperature. That's 98.6 degrees. It's known that hypothermia sets in if the body temp drops to 95 or below. Hypothermia can become more than a mere problem. It can kill you. Heaven knows, we don't need any more help in that department. So, bring on the sweater and the thick socks, I think I may be approaching 95.5.

One other element that can't be discounted. We don't get as much exercise as we once did. That affects blood flow ... and as we know now, temperature.

One older friend has a simple remedy. Eating. Having a full stomach helps to generate body heat. Calories, after all, are units of heat aren't they? There is a downside.

As we all know, overeating and the potential for weight gain creates its own set of problems. Obesity being the extreme outcome. That can cause some of the conditions we mentioned above. And, it can kill you. It's a Hobson's choice. Get fat and stay warm. Or ...

Anyone got a hot water bottle?

15: Feeling The Same at 25, Or 30, Or Even 50

Aside from the aches and pains and crankiness; aside from the medications and the need (read "necessity") to be in bed by 9:00 p.m., or, even aside from the general inability to leap tall buildings in a single bound (okay, I'm exaggerating here), why does my brain still think, in so many ways, as it did when I was twenty-five.

At twenty-five, there were no aches and pains. No medications (unless you count aspirin and Alka-Selzer), and changing routines was a way of life. There was perpetual good humor (unless one couldn't find an aspirin or Alka-Selzer). Leaping buildings in a single bound wasn't happening then either, but no other obstacles seemed insurmountable. Certainly not curbs. Life was good.

Getting older just meant more of the same. Until it didn't.

Nonetheless, I've never met contemporaries who do not wonder why he (and it's usually a "he" who has shared this with me) still thinks in many ways the way he did when much younger. He will readily admit still enjoying the figure of a pretty girl or young woman. Wistful though it may be. A relationship is clearly out of the question, but, my contemporaries say, you can always strike up a conversation with a pretty young thing by asking directions to the nearest 7-11, or for a recommendation for a good chiropractor. Even that is likely produce a cry for help, a frown, or an accusdation that you are "a dirty old man." As much as it might be pleasant to stop and chat with an attractive young woman under any pretext, proceed at your own risk. And, if she has a dog, don't proceed at all.

During my many walks in the local park, they come and go on foot, in-line skates, or bikes, many pushing baby carriages, but all showing off lithe and lean bodies amply displayed in halter tops and sexy short-shorts (there's the twenty-five-year-old again). Me? I'm the guy in sweats with black socks and white sneakers. Unfortunately, as soon as they spot the friendly elderly man (a.k.a. "aged letch"), out comes the cell phone. I'm convinced they're not talking to anyone, but they certainly want me to think they are.

Perhaps it's an excuse for not making eye contact, or it sends the message that they can hit the 911 buttons as soon as said letch makes a move. Any move. All I want to do is say hello, and advise them that if I were 50 years younger I'd be all over them. (Figuratively, of course.)

Which, sensing this, is why they show the phone. As a matter of fact, I do say "hello." Not only to the young ladies, but to everyone. Come to think of it, hardly anyone responds. Men, women, young or old.

Maybe it's the black socks.

You readers who are old enough, or young enough, to stay up late to watch old movies, might know the film *Gigi*, vintage 1958. It stared Leslie Caron and the famous French cabaret singer and entertainer, Maurice Chevalier. He played a character named Honore. One of his great numbers in the film is *Thank Heaven for Little Girls*. I'm tempted to break out into song whenever those "little girls" pass me in the park pretending to be on their cell phones where they can call for help in an instant if the old guy in sweats even so much as smiles at them.

By the way Chevalier has another song in *Gigi*. "I Remember it Well." He sang it in a duet with Mamita (Hermione Gingold). The pair, certainly in something resembling advanced years, think back on days of their youth when they had the kind of relationships many people do, especially in France. Their lives diverged; they moved on, but in this meeting, they reflect on what once was. They each "remember it well," but it seems she remembers much better than he. That includes virtually every detail, including the time, the place, the clothes they wore, the things they said. What they could agree on, was that they were once young and gay, that they were not getting old, and that he was a "prince of love in every way."

Fortunately, the music and lyrics, by Alan Jay Lerner and Frederick Loewe, live on. YouTube allows us to reminiscence one more time. Sigh.

As an aside, one interesting piece of trivia about Chevalier, who died in 1988. At the time of his death, he was the only living entertainer who had performed during the reign of every British monarch from Queen Victoria, up to and including Queen Elizabeth II. Victoria assumed the throne in 1837. But she ruled until 1901, the year then thirteen-year-old Chevalier began a professional entertainment career.

OK, OK, I digress.

During my walks in the park, there is another of those contradictions about the brain thinking it's still twenty-five when everything from the head down feels every bit of five decades more. My walks are about an hour long and cover about five miles. That's 1,700 hundred miles a year. In other words, I walk the equivalent from coast to coast every two years, and in the last fifteen years, I've walked around the world. Not bad.

But as I walk, I have become increasingly aware that just about everyone passes me by. Especially women. My pace is much faster than a stroll, but it's not a power walk. So why do women, and most men, have so little trouble putting me in their rearview mirror? Don't they know I have walked around the world? Of course, if I were a little faster I could do it in eleven or twelve years. God only knows how quickly I could get to California. But who's counting?

There are other things that cause our minds and bodies to play tricks as we age. One is the misplaced confidence that one's athleticism does not really change over time. Once an athlete, always an athlete. Take it from me, it's not true. I was once pretty good on the football field, tennis court, golf course, and racquetball court. As I think about it, I don't do any of those things anymore. It's not by choice (except for football). It's because I can't.

So now, I walk in the park. Except for when I fall. And, I seem to be doing that a lot. No, it's not the distraction of pretty girls. I have just begun to trip over things. A protruding tree root. An uneven sidewalk. Those dangerous curbs. No serious injuries. Yet. Lots of bruises. And some serious wounds to my pride.

I'm much more afraid of the bikers. Not the Hell's Angels. The boys and girls and men and women on bicycles who somewhat arrogantly want to convince the world that they are better than the rest of us by reducing their environmental footprint. I have found them collectively to be among the rudest of park visitors.

They come at you from all angles, speeding by in a blur and with an occasional, "On your left!" that scares the hell out of me and causes me to jump and almost trip over my own two feet.

They seem to think they own the pathways. Remember those little bells we used to all have on the handlebars of our bikes when we were kids? Needless to say, that was long before we ever heard about carbon footprints. They are way out of style with today's adult riders. I have never seen one or heard one used in the park. Unless the riders are shouting, "Get off the damn path!" as many of them do, they all too often prefer silence as they whisk up from behind and pass as close as they can to us walkers without actually striking those of us on foot. How ignominious it would be to suffer a serious injury by being struck by a bike. If it were a pretty girl who offered mouth-to-mouth resuscitation, however, it might be worth it.

16: Medicare, Medications, and Money

One of the things missing in today's world of media marketing is the fact that we older Americans have money to spend. We own our homes, and the kids are out of college. Medicare has kicked in. The 401ks are doing OK but could be better. Some of us, too, may also have pensions to supplement our income. And, there's always the funny apron brigade bringing in a few extra bucks as Walmart greeters.

Still, so many of us tend to spend what we have. That's why it's called "disposable income." And, we tend to dispose of it. Sometimes rather quickly Often on big-ticket items. Luxury cars, travel, grandkids.

I think this is something the media moguls have missed. They focus a lot of their advertising attention on the Millennials, you know, these young people still living at home, paying off college loans, and supporting at least one dog.

Advertisers target them because there are so many of them. Following traditional algorithms, they consider these kids low hanging fruit. They are the ones who will be buying cars, appliances, furniture, and homes. Eventually. Only huge numbers of these bright, stuck-in-place kids, are languishing in that basement. And, I hate to say it, waiting for an inheritance. Sometimes impatiently! OK, now, it's getting scary.

So, why aren't advertisers looking at us? *We* are the low handing fruit! We have all that disposable income. Oh, wait a minute; they are looking at us. Every evening … on the evening news … every disclaimer. But they aren't trying to sell us fancy cars or huge homes. They realize that a lot of that disposable income is going toward paying for medications. Count the number of ads focused on medications during the commercials. And they're encouraging it. Even with Medicare and the supplemental policies, medications can—and are—an out of pocket expense. You can do your own calculations.

I spend about $400 a month on medications. No senior discounts here. The pharmaceutical companies assure us that drugs are expensive because of all the time and money put into R&D (Research and Development). I'm not sure it's keeping me alive, or keeping my doctors in golf clubs, fancy dinners, or any of a number of perks pharmaceutical companies dole out to friendly physicians willing to prescribe their products. However, I am sufficiently terrified of the alternative that I dutifully write out the checks.

Anyone who has done any research on this will know that Big Pharma is reported to spend more on marketing than on R&D. That must tell us something.

There are also disturbing revelations that the drug companies have an interesting ploy when it comes to patents. Why? To keep their expensive products from stepping through the looking glass into the never-neverland of generic drugs. It's a profit killer. A slip of the wrist, and a tiny twist, and yesterday's formula for the big-ticket item can be sustained for another generation. All it takes is one tiny deviation from the original formula to make it a brand new product with a brand new, expanded life span.

Presto chango.

The fact is, many of us need the various medications to keep our hearts beating, our diabetes in check, our arthritis manageable, and all those other ailments under control. The only fly in the ointment is the stuff they are selling us for better health, can actually be harmful to our health. The TV ad disclaimers usually run longer than the other part of the commercial.

I know I don't want to spend my disposable windfall that I've worked my entire life to collect, on products that may cause, hallucinations, anxiety, vision problems, suicidal thoughts, confusion, extreme fear, hostility, urinary problems, oily discharge , etc.

Shudder.

Don't think for one minute that if such disclaiming information weren't required, it would be provided. Even with this indicting information, the TV ads are omnipresent (and expensive) as the drug companies implore their audience to "Ask your doctor if this is right for you." Is suicide right for you? Unusual bleeding? Oily discharge?

Hell, I've got enough problems without adding more. The mere thought of giving my hard-earned money to a billion-dollar pharmaceutical company, makes me hostile. I don't need a pill for that.

Fortunately, there's Medicare. It's the closest thing to universal coverage we are likely to have in our lifetime. Until you have to figure it out before you use it. Which can be a problem. Like learning about the donut hole and what it is, open enrollment, Medicare Advantage, plus so much more. Shoot, I barely knew what AARP was, but within moments of my fiftieth birthday AARP was on my case. Now, I'm a member. And that's only because they have been relentless in sending me stuff. And most of the time, they are simply trying to sell me something. Actually, I'm surprised there wasn't a courier at the front door at one minute after midnight on that birthday. I suspect, too, I'm not the only one they found who resents their constant nagging.

Also, I knew this was bound to happen. And, I also resented it as well—my first unsolicited senior citizen discount provided by a teenage cashier in a fast food joint. Yes, I was insulted, until I realized it was a *discount* and then realized that there are a lot of them out there. Be vigilant! So, I went from feeling insulted and embarrassed when I got that hamburger for 25 cents off the posted price to using my smart phone to find those senior discounts wherever I shop. Actually, I only do that when someone who knows how to do it on the phone is with me.

Now, one would think that spending about $400 a month on medications would indeed earn me a hefty senior discount. But who am I kidding? No senior discounts here.

17: Mirror, Mirror ...

The worst time of the day, every day for me is facing the mirror. At the outset, it would only be fair here to the mirror industry I suppose to point out that many of the unpleasant little discoveries we see in our reflection in no way is a reflection on them.

The scaly, crinkled, alligator-like skin that one day showed up on my forearms is a case in point. It has a name. It's crepey skin. Those crepe paper like crinkles showed up one day and no manner of oil or creams can erase them. I could show you a close up, but....

I confess that when I look in the mirror, I can't help but wonder if the high school or college beautiful people I once knew now look like me? Are their chin lines still square and firm? Are there wrinkles? Hair? And are the muscles that gave arms, legs, and torsos some definition now non-existent? Go to a 50th reunion and the answer will be obvious.

When we look at ourselves in the morning I believe most of us wonder who that person staring back at us actually is, and where did he or she come from?

My wife has the best line. From time to time, she stands before the mirror, looks at herself, and says, "Who is that bitch wearing my clothes?"

Like many women, she seems to prefer standing before a mirror in the dark and covering her face with her hands. I don't know why; she's gorgeous.

When staring back at the man looking back at me, I can only speak for myself and maybe some men in general, but there are a few things that jump out at me:

My hair! Where the hell did that go? Why can't I be one of those guys who still have a full head of hair? What did they do to deserve that? Is it just genetic? Thanks, Mom. Or is it simply proof that an overabundance of testosterone has fled this aging body?

Just so you know, some of us guys do worry a lot about receding hairlines. Which has led to a couple of limp and overused explanations.

"No grass grows on a busy street."

"My head is a solar panel for a sex machine."

Hah! The wife will get a good laugh, or cry, over that one.

Before we get off the subject of hair, there is a point that must be made about the comb over. Don't.

Combing hair from one side of the head to the other,

over a broad bald spot is not aesthetically pleasing. At least in my book. But in all things, there is a redeeming quality. For instance, when, in a brisk wind, the hair lifts off and stands straight up, observers are entertained by the comic interlude. Of course, this is spoken by someone with no hair to comb over!

One thing about this, though. Women aren't off the hook. Many find themselves with thinning hair, too, and perhaps a bald spot right on the crown of the head. And that is probably a bigger deal with women than it is with men. Well, maybe not. At least when we decide to shave our heads, it's the 'in' thing to do. Women, I'm not so sure.

And what is it with women and their hair in general? Among the first things I've heard women say to other women is, "I love your hair," or "What have you done to your hair?" I've never told a man, "Great comb-over," or "Who's your barber? I just have to have him do my hair." I'd probably be mincemeat.

And shoes? Do all women have a love affair with shoes? And purses?

I just thought of something. Maybe when I see a pretty girl while walking in the park, I can smile and say, "I love your hair!" or "Where did you get those shoes? I must have a pair!"

OK, I'll stop before I really get myself into trouble.

So, let's move back to wrinkles. All I can say is that they, like s**t, happens. But you know that. One day, when

I asked an older, black colleague of mine why his face was as smooth as a baby's, he responded, "Black don't crack." I certainly can't attest to that, but if what he says is true, for all the things that blacks have been denied in this world, that may be God's payback. Not enough, for sure, but it's a really good start.

Some like to call wrinkles laugh lines, or emblematic of some other pleasant personality trait. It's always a "pleasant" trait. Except when it's not.

Those pouches that puff up on the sides of the face have nothing to do with humor, or a pleasing personality. Instead, they may really have more to do with eating and drinking too much. And yes, getting old. Geez. Do I have to keep saying it?

Once I heard that generous swabs of Preparation-H can tighten skin and thereby erase wrinkles. As appealing as the supposed outcome would be, I just can't make myself go there. There's only one place for Preparation-H, and it's not on the face!

Another thing I found when standing and looking at myself in the mirror. It's best to stand some distance from the mirror. Otherwise more unpleasantness comes to light. Nose hairs. And, of course, ear hairs.

I've known men who could let that hair grow, use it as a creative comb over to lose that bald look. That would give everyone a good chuckle. Chuckle, hell, that would merit and outright guffaw.

Alright. I'll change the subject. Just remember, "Bald is better."

I realize that the ladies are not immune to this extraneous hair issue that sometimes crops up along their chin. Again, "Bald is better."

Which leads me to the subject of beards. I've noticed a tendency with some gentlemen at a certain age, to suddenly decide that it might be a good idea to grow a beard.

This is well and good. Some men take on a bit of a debonair look with a beard. Unfortunately, one cannot always be sure that the beard will grow out in the same color as the hair on their head, if they have any. If an older man's hair still has color (in other words, not gray), the beard may not follow suit. Does this mean the fellow dyes his hair? Men don't do that, do they? Young men who grow beards are often shocked when their facial hair grows out in a funky shade of red or blonde. That's highly unlikely for oldsters. More than likely, the beard will probably be some variation of your sideburns. Or ear hair.

Speaking of dying the hair, I now know there are various products on the market to darken one's hair ... either on the head or the face. You've no doubt seen the commercials featuring once prominent athletes who use various products to darken beards. Nice try. Nothing looks more artificial than coal dark facial hair on a septuagenarian. Don't be fooled by the thirty-something chicks who seem drawn to them, even amorously so in the TV commercials. They're pretty convincing until the camera shuts down. You've got to know they run to their dressing rooms to throw up after all that on camera cuddling, snuggling, and fondling that is clearly as artificial as the dye itself.

Let's face it. The beard that suddenly emerges in one's advanced years is not designed to attract younger women. The reason, I believe, is generally one of vanity. As previously suggested, time and gravity have a way of producing double chins and jowls. What better way to cover them, and perhaps a few unsightly blemishes, than with a generous beard or stylish goatee?

Yes, old folks can be narcissistic, too. And vain.

Then there is that other type of 'vein'. The exploding kind. On the nose, the cheeks. We call them veins, but they are actually arteries. Or maybe capillaries. I forget. If they were veins, they might look like those ropes on your legs. So, they're one of the smaller things. I'll Google it. When my daughter comes to visit.

They—whatever they are—could possibly be the result of the aforementioned eating and drinking. Or, maybe just thinning skin. Have we talked about that before? Oh yes, now I remember. It has something to do with time, as in age, reducing the fat layer below the skin. And making us cold.

As to the hair growing in the nose and ears. Where the heck is that coming from? The hair on the head is long gone. Hair on the legs and chest is gone. But the hair that grows in the other places as we age is on steroids. There must be one or two drops of testosterone left in the old vessel after all. It's just misdirected, as well as insufficient. Science must look into this. Are there no longer older scientists who have a vested interest in finding a cure and putting some of that hair back where it belongs? Like on our heads. And what about you younger scientists? Don't kid yourself. Your day is coming!

And while you guys are at it, figure out that "black don't crack" puzzle. Inquiring minds want to know!

Moving down the line, another image that is not lost during the morning mirror inspection is the noticeable lack of muscle mass. It's not the only mass that disappears of course, but where do those muscles go? They certainly don't stay put. The arms get skinny and lack definition (there's that word again). And along with the transformation, goes our strength. Opening a bottle of pickles can be a challenge requiring implements the likes of which NASA would be proud.

And why is it that shoulders that once were broad and wider than our waistline, are suddenly the same size? In some cases, the waistline wins the contest.

Then, along with all the other changes, sometimes you notice something new gracing your face, your arms, legs. It's not the liver spot. We know about those. No, this is something that is always discovered with the same kind of surprise as finding that other person staring back at you in the mirror. And, of course, as you fondly remember those glorious sun-scorching summers on the Jersey shore, comes an immediate suspicion, so you take a closer look. Is that … are those … cancerous? Then you strip down and do a complete once over and find those funny little brown scaly growths have popped up on, well, everywhere.

So, one heads to a dermatologist. Been to a dermatologist lately? They are not cheap. Even with Medicare … if they take Medicare.

On this first time around, the doctor burns them off after assuring the patient, "Oh, it's nothing. I see these all the time." The next time they show up, you just live with them.

So far, I have been sharing my observations and internal thoughts that come before me in a *small* mirror. You know, the one on the medicine cabinet. That pretty much covers the top half of the body. But, there is an entirely different dynamic when I stand in front of the full-length version.

My best advice? Whenever and however possible, avoid this version. Especially if your lighting is fluorescent. Do not … I repeat … do not do it. *Do not do it*. Everything that is bad, is made worse. Much worse. Soft lighting is the only way to go in any room in which there is a mirror. It ain't pretty to see all that sagging, wrinkled skin, and atrophied muscle presented in one package framed by thinning, graying hair, and anchored by swollen ankles. No selfies here, thank you very much.

Even better ... candles! Better yet. Brush your teeth, and even shave in the dark.

18: The Media

If it weren't for the amount of advertising Big Pharma does on television (disclaimers and all), it wouldn't be difficult to assume that today's media are hell bent on ignoring older Americans. Watching the evening news is like looking at the ghost of Christmas future. The array of medications we are either taking, or likely to take at some point, is a glimpse into the future. And, it's about the only way programmers will acknowledge that we are out there at all, unless they come up with a sitcom with an unflattering story line about older Americans. It's not smart.

There are certainly exceptions, but older Americans have the money, even with the Great Recession. The house is paid for and the kids are out of college. As mentioned earlier, many of us have sold the empty nest and acquired a nice nest egg. Add to that the Social Security, pensions, and 401k. And unless that all has been squandered, or health issues have claimed a chunk of it (and we do have Medicare), we have significant disposable income. And, we spend it. On big cars, luxury trips and restaurants. You name it. I'm not certain why we are not targeted even more by advertisers wanting to get their hands on some of that buying power.

Maybe it's because of the way we are portrayed on television and many movies. Older folks are generally portrayed as being in the way, old fashioned, cheap, dependent on their kids, and a little bit looney. They are early to bed, late to rise, frugal, warm milk drinking has beens in their dotage. In short, by and large, a nuisance, better not to be seen nor heard.

Television is primarily geared to the Millennials. I hope the reception's good in the basement. The assumption is that they are the consumers of the future. As mentioned before, they will be buying the big-ticket items, the cars, the refrigerators, the houses, and the sophisticated electronics. And they will. Let's not forget the economy of recent years has not been kind to them. They are having trouble finding good jobs. When they do, for the most part they don't pay all that well or offer the kinds of benefits we older folk relied on. They have more college debt than the amount the entire country owes on credit cards and auto loans.

We are assumed to be clueless when it comes to pop-culture, unaware of John Stewart, Jimmy Kimmel,

Jimmy Fallon, and Stephen Colbert. Okay, there may be something to that. After all, they do come on after 9:30. While we may pay less attention to Beyoncé, Kanye West, or Lady Gaga, it doesn't mean we're not with it. It means we like the music and entertainment of our era better, just as today's younger generation will like theirs better than the things their kids will be listening and laughing to down the road.

I get it. I think we would have a hard time convincing our kids and grandkids to find some of what we liked very palatable. Eyes roll when talk turns to Bing Crosby and, sometimes, even Bob Dylan. *TV Guide* recently proclaimed the old *Ed Sullivan* TV show as one of the 50 best television shows of all time. Try describing that show to today's younger set and get ready for the yawns. Radio also has little interest to today's younger set. They can't seem to relate to the notion of listening to an hour-long radio drama, as we did. Even if it starred the biggest stars of an era. I don't get much reaction when I mention Orson Welles sending a large chunk of the Northeast population, and other places, into mass hysteria with a realistic version of *War of the Worlds*. Hell, Beyoncé can do that leaving (or going to) a restaurant.

People in New York and New Jersey took to the streets on foot and in their cars when Welles reported on the eve of World War II that Martians had landed in Grover's Mill, New Jersey. The people of Grover's Mill put a significant number of bullets into a local water tower thinking it was a Martian Space ship. Maybe Martians will do the same when we start landing people on the red planet.

Perhaps members of today's generation don't need radio's "theater of the mind." Watching the reality of 9/11, mass shootings, and many subsequent events may send make-believe to the back of the bus.

Here's a Freudian segue. It has to do with political correctness. Something that evolved with us as we aged and became somewhat more enlightened. You'd be hard-pressed to find many people who would argue against the demise of the old *Amos 'n' Andy* television show. *Amos 'n' Andy* was a sitcom about black characters set in Harlem. Lots of stereotyping in the series with characters named Kingfish, Sapphire, and Lightnin'. The TV series lasted two years, from 1951 to 1953. A far cry from the radio program that inspired it. Here are some basic facts about the radio program.

To begin with, *Amos 'n' Andy* was the 1928 creation of two white men: Freeman Gosden and Charles Correll. They played all the main roles, including the women—all black.

The fifteen-minute program aired nightly from 1928 to 1943, when the show was expanded to thirty minutes. That one ran until 1955. More than 4,000 episodes in all. It's estimated the nightly program reached forty million listeners—one-third of the country's population. For a quarter of a century, white America tuned in and grew fond of the characters and their lives. But, by the mid-fifties, not coincidentally, the Brown v. Board of Education Supreme Court decision came to pass and the show was considered too much for too many. The country was changing. So, the show was cancelled, ending an era, in radio at least. The only sitcom comparable to the popularity of the American public was *The Cosby Show* and the Huxtable family. That came thirty years after *Amos 'n' Andy* signed off.

An author's note here. I recently listened to a recording of the program that aired on Christmas Eve in 1941, less than a month after Pearl Harbor. The dialogue was spoken as the world was going to war. In it, the character Amos, in the context of the time, explains the Lord's Prayer line by line to his daughter. The recording was extraordinarily moving. It's hard to imagine anyone would have found that episode politically incorrect.

It's hard to imagine, too, that a program like *Amos 'n' Andy* could get off the storyboard today. But facts are facts. And history is history, and this hugely popular radio program is credited with having created the template for countless radio and television sitcoms that followed, including those that are more politically correct, and that, perhaps, have contributed to a better understanding of racial divisiveness, its causes, and to bridging the divide. The surge of podcast popularity may bring back the theater of the mind. It is the younger generation's "radio."

19: Dressing

If it weren't for the gray hair, the wrinkles, and the varicose veins, the one feature that sets us older humans apart is often the way we dress. It's called "mix and mismatch." Nothing like a plaid shirt with patterned Bermuda shorts. Nothing like sheer, black, over the calf socks with those same shorts. Throw on a pair of laced-up black shoes and one is ready for the beach or the park. It has become a favored look, among others. No wonder the grandkids tag along either way in front of us, or so far behind, we think we've lost them. If they even agree to come along with us. And forget about asking them if they want to bring a friend along.

You would think that a lifetime of getting dressed every day would actually make us better dressers. For some inexplicable reason, it has not. The only excuse for some of the clothes (perhaps costumes is a better word), we venture into public wearing is due to severe vision impairment, up to, and including blindness. Our significant others might be expected, even counted on, to correct the sartorial mistake. Unless, that is, they quite possibly have a similar problem. The fact remains, however, that how we dress can easily generate gales of laughter from strangers and loved ones alike. Or maybe it generates waves of pity from those who fear dementia has begun to set in.

For some reason, the famous photograph of Richard Nixon walking on a beach dressed in a three piece suit and dress shoes as the surf splashed a few feet away comes to mind. Nixon was not yet in advanced years, but he was probably around sixty. The photo was taken to show that the president was just like everyone else. Except, of course, for those who prefer to walk along the surf line in shorts or a bathing suit. Or barefoot.

Perhaps he was, please pardon the expression, in something like a "dress rehearsal" for the forthcoming dotage. Lord knows he had plenty of people who might have told him that it was not the best possible photo op. Given the former president's tendency to not always listen to best advice, one can imagine him saying something like, "Others may hate you. But those who hate you don't win, unless you hate them. And then, you destroy yourself."

Oh, wait a minute, he did say that. It was August 9, 1974 as he was flying off to California in disgrace, and also in what appeared to be the same suit he'd worn for his walk on the beach.

Again, I've gone off on a tangent.

I'm guessing here, but I suspect one of the reasons old folks don't worry about what they wear is just that. They don't worry about it. They are not trying to impress anyone. It's not like they're going to a singles bar to pick up a hot chick. We're more likely to be going to the local Walgreens to pick up some milk of magnesia. Or Depends.

If I may be permitted this aside, worrying about how we look with clothes on is of much, much less concern than what we look like with our clothes off. That IS something to be concerned about.

Actually, it is a big plus to cover up our aging bodies. Clothes is the only a means of covering up all the bumps, bruises, rashes, exploding veins, flabby bellies, and other blemishes that have found residence in aging bodies. There is, of course, a small percentage of us who are indeed heading for that singles bar, however. If the plaid-on-plaid look is bad on one end of the sartorial spectrum, on the other end, the "I'm trying to look like I'm thirty" is a disaster. Chains, tight pants, leather, dyed hair, you name it, trying to dress young when you're not, does not work.

Don't do it.

Other signs we have crossed the Rubicon and have left youth and middle age on the other side:

- Mismatched socks.
- Sagging stockings.
- Suspenders actually used to hold up trousers.

- Trousers that are too short (because of tight suspenders) exposing the mismatched socks.
- Trousers hitched well above the waist.
- Stains on shirts, sweaters, and ties, invariably from a previous era, or eras.
- Sweaters with holes in them, either from moths, or from cigarette burns from way back when he or she smoked.
- Shoes that are more sensible than stylish, usually that do not require laces.
- Tennis shoes.
- Unzipped zippers.
- Patterned sports coats that are a complete mismatch for the accompanying patterned shirts and patterned ties. Think checkered coat, plaid shirt, boldly-striped tie, perhaps topped off with a fedora from 1955.

You get the idea. There are some other areas where style can get away from us older folks.

Men, no Speedos. Ladies, no tights or halter tops.

Another area of potentially making a fool of oneself comes at holiday times. Older people should be careful of donning Santa hats at Christmas, or bunny suits at Easter. Resist any temptation to wear a Pilgrim's hat, or a politically-incorrect Indian headdress, at Thanksgiving. Dressing entirely in red on Valentine's Day can work. If there aren't too many stains.

I do want to note that particular care should be taken at Halloween. There is often a temptation to relive our earliest days by finding a costume to entertain kids, or to go to neighborhood parties. Almost nothing works. Just leave it at that.

My wife and I go to a neighbor's home every Halloween. He's a contemporary. It's the host's favorite holiday and he encourages costumes. He usually wears bib overalls and calls himself a farmer, which he once was. So, he's really only in what was once his business suit. Still.

Some of the older guests do show up in various outfits, usually running from the ridiculous to the utterly ridiculous. Believe me, there is nothing that works for a seventy-five-year-old man in a Superman costume. For that matter, a woman of the same vintage masquerading as an acrobat or ballet dancer doesn't work, either.

My wife and I go sans-costume and simply identify ourselves as "an elderly gentlemen with his trophy wife." At least that's what I say. I shudder to think what she tells folks. And no, I never ask.

The one thing I've learned about clothing as I've gotten older is to wear a bright shirt or sweater if you haven't shaved, or have bloodshot or rheumy eyes. People are less likely to notice the oversight or imperfections. Another tip, too. Wearing dark shirts or sweaters makes one look thinner, as do vertical stripes. White does just the opposite. Many mornings, the toughest decision of the day, when one has not shaved or when eyes are bloodshot, is whether to divert attention from those less-than-dreamy eyes or how to look thin. What a way to start the day.

Having said all that, there are some of my generation who have a sense of style and look as though they just stepped out of a fashion magazine. They dress in "outfits" that are crisp, new, and stain free—and that fit. Admittedly, folks like this are an exception. I strongly suspect someone is dressing them. Probably a son or daughter, or a grandchild who has been embarrassed once too often.

For the younger readers who have stayed with me here, I would caution against being too quick to laugh at oldsters because of the way they dress. We all know that some kids, and some even beyond youth, have been known to make fun of old people. For them, I would suggest they see the movie *Saving Private Ryan*, if only for the first twenty minutes or so. That's the striking scenes of the Normandy landing on D-Day. I was moved to write this on a recent Veteran's Day.

I can remember World War II. Rationing. Propaganda. Neighbors not coming home. I have seen countless war movies and have also seen "Victory at Sea." I've read Stephen Ambrose and others, not to mention Stephen Crane and Barbara Tuchman, with their graphic detail on other wars.

Ever wonder how you would stand up under fire? Ever made fun of an old man or woman walking down the street? He's in shorts and long black socks. She's in wrinkled stockings slipping down her legs. Maybe there's too much hair growing out of his ears and her chin. Maybe they couldn't hear or see too well.

Talking to themselves?

Could be.

Comic, right?

Time to remember who they are and who they were. They were there at Omaha Beach, or Pork Chop Hill, or Hue. Maybe even in the Brooklyn Naval Yard building the battleship Missouri.

Wherever. They were there. Contributing. And we are here now, and speaking English, not German; not Japanese. We're here because that old guy, or old gal, stormed the beach, or danced with a guy who died tomorrow.

Everyone should remember why we should have respect for that old fellow holding up the line at the Post Office, or the woman cramming thirteen items into the twelve-item express lane at the local supermarket.

Next time that makes you mad, think about who they are … and what they did … before those who are laughing were born.

20: Late-in-Life Marriage

I'm certain there are empirical studies that would show that men are more inclined to remarry after the death of a spouse than women. Especially older men. In the interest of saving time and searching Google for such studies, I will rely instead on anecdotal evidence. My own father took less than a year to remarry after the death of my mother. They had been married thirty years. His new wife was thirty years his junior.

Women seem be less eager to find a new mate. Certainly not within the few months of the death of a spouse. Is it that they feel to do so would amount to some sort of betrayal to the departed mate? It could also represent a mindset of "been there, done that. Let's get on and live our lives and have some fun." I know a lot of widows who do just that. Why not? More power to them. And there are a lot of them. Women do outlive men by a fair margin. Four years on average. That gap is closing as more women work and experience workforce stresses, while men are engaged in less physical labor than was once was the case.

Let's also not forget that because of the gap, there are fewer men out there for older women. That either drives women to the Caribbean cruise or the tour bus, or puts them in the market for a younger man. Getting into that would take me into waters with which I am not familiar. Let's assume, however, that women of almost any age don't find that an unattractive option. Same for men. Only more so. I think. Again, I'm making certain assumptions, but I think there are more trophy wives out there than trophy husbands. Sorry ladies. I wish men lived longer to give you an equal shot at a "trophy."

It seems that almost without exception when men rush to the alter after the death of their wives, they are somehow considered guilty of infidelity, even in a post-mortem context. Especially when they marry a younger woman. I admit to something close to that in my own family. I, and people like me, wonder out loud as to "How could he?" Well, there are a couple of plausible explanations.

One is that if a man has an opportunity to hook up with an attractive younger woman, this lines up nicely with the lifelong tendency of man at any age to have a "looker" on his arm. A few bucks in the bank doesn't hurt that option, either. While it would be unfair to characterize all May to September marriages or relationships in that way, it would be folly to deny that it does happen. Sometimes to the extreme. Dick Van Dyke's wife is forty-six years younger than the ninety-year-old entertainer.

But, now, it's time to get to the nitty gritty. There is a very clear reason to me as to why men remarry, and remarry quickly. Again, sorry for the big reveal guys. Basically, it's because we men are so dependent on women. (Reminder. I'm writing this from a man's perspective.)

While men pride themselves as those macho beings who don't need help doing anything, the die is cast during our working lives. While baby boomers and we pre-boomers were out earning a living … and let's face it, most of our generation worked outside the home while the women stayed home and took care of business in their own way. She tended to the kids, did the shopping, and made minor repairs. If she could not make those repairs she called someone who could. The plumbers, electricians, and general handymen were in her Rolodex. That Rolodex was often in her head rather than on paper. She may even have been responsible for handling family finances. Even though they may not have worked outside the home, work they did. Work many men would fail to do—or master.

The man of the house would come home after his day at work and things had been taken care of. If children had been sick, the wife had taken care of them herself, or found the doctor who did. If the kids had to be picked up from school, she did it. If the car failed, she had it fixed. She also managed the grocery shopping, the laundry, fixed dinner, washed the dishes, then listened to "him" explain to her what a rough day he had had at the office.

On that sad occasion when she pre-deceases him, he is left without the Rolodex, or the first clue as to whom to call in those emergencies. This is often exacerbated when the surviving husband is older. He might be in his seventies and have no clue as to who the plumber or electrician is. He doesn't know how to shop for groceries, and even has less of an idea as to how to cook at all, much less cook for one. More than likely, he'll opt for a local diner or the artery clogging greasy spoon. Or even worse, the neighborhood bar. And as for the laundry? Forget it.

He suddenly realizes that he is at a loss as to how to go about the day-to-day business of managing his life, or a household.

As a widower, he may not realize, perhaps until it's too late, the role she played in demanding that he see a doctor when various ailments surfaced. If it were up to men, they would never go to the doctor because whatever it is that's bothering him will take care of itself, or go away after time. A lot of men's lives have no doubt been saved by wives who badger their husbands into seeing a doctor. Or who take it upon themselves to make an appointment for him.

Adding to all this is the loneliness factor. After a lifetime of having someone there, that someone suddenly isn't. What then? As days, weeks, and months slowly pass, there comes the realization that the friends that he and his wife had known and seen over the years, were really more her friends than his. She was the social director. He may find it difficult to maintain the relationships without her. The realization inevitably surfaces that those friends liked her more than him, and that she was the glue that kept everyone and everything together. A certain desperation vies with a growing depression that while he was earning the daily bread, she ran the household and everything that went with it. The great awakening is that he doesn't know how to survive without her. And that he is not very good at it anyway.

The first holidays without her would be excruciating, as they would be for women having lost a husband. Women of our generation, however, are actually better equipped to move on and manage themselves and a household because of having done so all of their lives. They are generally more social and make friends more easily than men.

Little wonder that surveys show that more than fifty percent of older, recently widowed men are in a new relationship within a year of the spouse's death. The surveys indicate men are six or seven times more likely than women to begin a new relationship, and five times more likely to remarry. That may be due in part because women outlive men, and there are fewer men for women to marry.

Needless to say, the new relationship brings with it a fair measure of guilt. And criticism. Kids are often stunned to think that Dad could find comfort with someone else within months (or sometimes years) after Mom's death. Friends of the former couple often react the same way. All see the new relationship as a form of betrayal. Guilt is also not lost on the surviving spouse.

The case can be made that it is less betrayal than a form of loyalty. That new relationship can be interpreted as evidence of the strength of the previous union, showing not only the widower's commitment to his marriage, but how dependent he was on her in every way.

21: Family Histories

Are your kids or grandkids asking questions? Do they want to know about your life, or about the lives of your parents and grandparents? If they don't, you can only blame yourself, because you probably didn't, either.

And now, how many times have you regretted not having done so?

There are some who might argue that if there is any such thing as eternal life, it may only be "eternal" for as long as the memory of ancestors is retained by surviving generations. For that to happen histories must be passed down. That may include family stories passed along through photographs, journals, genealogies, memoires, recordings, and the like.

Many of these mementos offer wonderful opportunities to maintain accurate accounts of family. If one is inclined not to be accurate, it is also an opportunity to gild the family lily. Though I'm not encouraging this, it is admittedly hard to resist a certain amount of embellishment. For instance:

- Did grandfather Clem rival Alvin York's World War I exploits in WW II?
- Did uncle Bill really rival Alvin York's World War I exploits in Korea?
- Did Dad really rival Audie Murphy's World War II exploits in Vietnam?
- Was great grandfather Orvis really Alvin York?
- Was great aunt Millie really Rosie the Riveter?
- Was your grandmother really often mistaken for Grace Kelly?
- Did your mother really date Marlon Brando?

But who has time to compile the histories? Well, actually, we all do. If we give it some thought. Holidays and family gatherings offer wonderful opportunities. There are organizations that encourage preservation of family stories. NPR's *StoryCorps* provides a pretty good template. Of course, in this day and age, *StoryCorps* even has an app to make passing along family history and stories easier.

Many of these organizations have a more local or regional focus and encourage young people to ask questions and make audio or video recordings of the answers of their older relatives. Often they are then encouraged to also write those stories.

Many stories are sent to various archives, including the Library of Congress, where one day they will be presumably be read by historians. Or voyeurs.

Let's get real. It's hard to imagine who will be interested a hundred years from now about Uncle Jed's club foot, or when great aunt Mathilda had twins. But, we never know.

The key to making this work and to provide information that is both informative and valuable is that one has to learn to answer questions that will produce that kind of information. Remember, this may all wind up in an archive that can be accessed by anyone.

Fair warning. When a precocious twelve year old approaches with a tape recorder firmly in hand, and a paper containing a long list of questions such as those below, be wary. Especially if you've had a stiff blackberry brandy to ward off the seasonal chill.

So, it might be well to keep in mind questions that should *not* be answered, much less asked. Some examples.

- Did you ever have an abortion?
- Did you ever have a sexually transmitted disease?
- Why do you hate blacks? Hispanics? Asians? The Irish? Jews? Italians? Catholics? Mormons? Protestants?
- Did you ever commit adultery?
- Were you ever in prison?
- Are there any relatives you dislike?
- Are you a Communist?
- Did you contribute to Donald Trump's campaign?

You get the idea.

Although it probably isn't necessary, I do want to point out that questions such as these are not likely to be answered honestly. So, there is probably no point in anyone asking them in the first place, except for the fact that the answers, honestly responded to or not, can be quite entertaining. So, if you want to be the entertainer, have at it with tongue firmly in cheek. Don't forget, however, that the humor may not go over so well if the tape winds up in the Library of Congress to be listened to fifty years later by someone writing a family history. Who knows, that precocious twelve year old might run for president one day, when journalists and opponents will gleefully pounce on such potentially damaging information about lineage. If that happens, you will likely be dead. (See Mortality). But, you certainly don't want the grandkid to be denied the White House, so you must calculate very, very, very carefully. On the other hand, if you're dead, what the hell.

If you really want to have some fun, and have been subjected to one of the "elder interviews," engage in a little payback with the interviewer. Ask them questions from the list just above. It can be especially amusing if you ask the questions at the Thanksgiving, Christmas, or Kwanza dinner tables. Or at the Passover Seder.

22: Losing Dignity, or Ignorance is Bliss

If I still have the eyes of the younger set here. This is for you. There is an unfair number of ways to lose dignity as one ages. While our own recognition of the things that erode our dignity may be faulty, rest assured that others do notice and discuss it (albeit, at times, secretly. Or at least out of earshot).

Even by those who love us most. Or profess to.

These less than dignified occurrences can, and often do, lead to outright banishment at the worst, and grudging acceptance at best. Throw in being shunned at times, laughed at, and/or given that "Oh no, not again" look, and it's enough to make one tremble with anger and hurt.

A word of caution. Trembling is a bad reaction. It may be seen as your inability to maintain composure, or take things in stride. It can also lead to an amateur diagnosis of early onset Parkinson's which can land you somewhere you don't want to be.

To be unaware of those dignity sappers can be something of a blessing. That's where the expression, "Ignorance is bliss" fits in very nicely. While it is best to actually be ignorant, it is perfectly acceptable for older people to *pretend* to be ignorant. Or joke about it.

A warning is in order here. The jokes you think are funny may not play well, or be funny to relatives and friends. For instance. Drooling. What's funny about drooling? Especially at the dinner table, or during an animated conversation with friends, and even more so with strangers. Still, even as we grow older, we need a good laugh now and again.

Seriously, though, what's funny about what I call occasional "leakage?" Some call it "spotting." That's the telltale wet spot on the trousers caused by an inadvertent pee spurt that occasionally comes out of nowhere without warning. Well, it's not technically out of nowhere is it? That's why so many of the male senior set have taken to wearing dark trousers. Leakage is a particular problem for men who have had prostate surgery.

Let me caution you to be most circumspect about letting people know if you are wearing diapers. Few things are more subject to ridicule. It ain't funny folks! Yet, more and more older people, and some younger ones, have to wear Depends, or something like Depends, because of surgery or physical issues that cause some level of incontinence.

But just imagine the ridicule, not to mention disdain, of having to navigate the day without that protection. "Leakage" is one thing, but a deluge is quite another. And that's not even bringing a renegade BM (you figure it out) into the picture. Not a pretty picture indeed. Losing dignity is one thing. Humiliation is quite another.

A further humiliation beyond wearing diapers is purchasing the damn things. It would be possible to send an emissary to make the purchase, but that requires acknowledgement to someone that they are necessary. Which is what one seeks to avoid. No, this is a chore consumers must do for themselves, and thereby suffer the humiliation when we present the package with its huge bright lettering before a cute, twenty-something cashier at the checkout counter. God forbid you have to ask someone in the store where to find them. I can hear the manager using the speaker system now: "Customer needs help finding Depends." One can compare it all to the embarrassment of a teenager, or even an adult, furtively purchasing condoms. The comparison is strikingly apt.

Let's move on. Nothing inspires a good chuckle like a resounding fart. Unless, of course, it is your own. No one laughs when Grandpa or Grandma does it, unless it's behind their back (pun intended). There is no good way to explain it away. The only positive note, is that young kids sometimes ... strike that ... *always* think it's funny. However, their laughter does nothing to restore any level of dignity. There is one way, though, to try and save face. You lean in close to the kid and say, "I did that on purpose, you know. Just for the fun of it." This might play well with the kids, but not always with adults. Above all, don't try and make your point by trying to squeeze another one out. You just might wish you were wearing Depends.

The fact is that there is nothing funny about losing one's dignity. Anyone who has ever had dealings with someone who has been forbidden to drive knows what that means. I can only imagine the loss of independence is crushing when the car keys are taken away. Crushing, I might add, for those who lose the privilege, and for those who take the keys away. Exchanging places with parents as the decision maker and caregiver cannot be easy.

There's nothing funny, either, about needing care and having to rely on caregivers for the most basic of needs. What greater humiliation and loss of dignity can there be in having to be assisted in matters of the toilet? When one can't feed him or herself, that, too, has serious consequences for one's self-respect and self-worth.

Something else that may seem like a little thing, but the inability to keep up when walking with a younger person also takes a toll. It is further evidence that time is marching on, when you, increasingly, can't. At least not at an equal pace. And that sucks.

Then there is an issue of communication. Sometimes older people have a difficult time making themselves understood. Something happens to the larynx when people age. Vocal cords stretch. The voice becomes weaker. Imagine the frustration after a loved one suffers a stroke. It can be all but impossible to formulate a coherent sentence, or one that anyone can hear.

There is one area that robs one of one's dignity, and is particularly cruel. That's the dismissive attitude many people assume when dealing with older people who don't walk well, hear well, remember well, or who have difficulty making themselves readily understood. They are often dealt with impatiently, if they are dealt with at all. Too many people have little difficulty sluffing older people off, as if they didn't exist at all. I remember one elderly woman who was all but ignored by a salesperson in a not-so-busy store. The older woman finally said, "Why aren't you waiting on me? After all … I am a person!" Her words won a condescending smile, but no service as the sales lady moved to another customer. I don't shop there anymore.

Yes, another word of warning. This one to the younger set who find it convenient to be dismissive, impolite, and inattentive to the older set. Rethink it. One day, you'll be standing where we are.

The first loss of dignity may be that day within seconds of one's fiftieth birthday when one receives the invitation from the AARP, the American Association of Retired Persons. But you already know that. You are asked to join and revel in all the benefits offered, many of which are insurance-related. Those of you (us) who can remember back to age fifty, may recall the feeling of insult that you (we) have now been categorized in some databank as an "older" person.

It may not occur to many that this whole idea is a marketing project. And, a brilliant one. Lots of discounts and pathways to products that are attractive to us as we age. However, it is, for some, at worst, insulting. At best, it is demoralizing to receive that passport to senior status. No one wants to be reminded that the sands of time are slipping through the hourglass.

But wait a minute. What's wrong with discounts and saving money? (see Parsimony) Maybe I should expand on this discussion. We may not find it necessary to become a card-carrying member of AARP in order to take advantage of many money-saving opportunities. There are all sorts of senior discounts available. They are not especially well advertised, but ask for one, or at least ask if any are available anywhere you do business.

I remember going into a fast food place when I was about fifty. I ordered the usual artery clogging, heart stopping, fat-and-cholesterol-laden special of the day, and pulled out a few bills and some loose change to pay. The kid at the counter had enough pimples to play connect the dots. (Have you noticed that many of the kids at fast food counters have bad complexions? That should tell us something. Not about the kids. About the food.) She said something like, "That's $4.75. But, with the senior discount, it's $4.10."

I was instantly outraged. How dare she? I'm a long way from senior discount world, I thought. I was about to suggest she invest in a tube of Clearasil. (Do they still make that stuff, or are skin problems now handled with lasers?) And I was about to ask for a supervisor and send this kid back to her home economics class when it occurred to me that the operative word was not Clearasil, but discount!

My blood pressure subsided and I graciously accepted the benevolence of MacDonald's or Burger King ... whatever it was, and pulled out four ones and a quarter. I was tempted to leave her a fifteen-cent tip, but thought better of it. (See Parsimony)

Then I skipped out of the joint, greasy bags in hand, happily on with the mission of inviting triple-bypass surgery.

23: Fear

Does everyone who is lucky enough to achieve old age also see fear levels increase? Of course there is the fear of dying. Don't be fooled by those who say they don't fear it. You might hear them say something like, "It's just the next chapter." "Everyone dies." "I'm tired." "I don't fear it." "I'm eager to meet God and see heaven."

Nope. People fear dying, and give it away with pitiful and pithy comments designed to distract from and deflect impressions that they are fearful of the Grim Reaper. In fact, they are a prayer-like form of mendicant behavior.

"I just want to live long enough to see my grandchildren."

"I want to see my grandson graduate from high school."

"I want to be at my granddaughter's wedding." To that, one might reply, "You will be … but as an angel. At least you won't have to pay for it."

And, while we're on the subject, be suspicious of any spouse who says they hope their surviving husband or wife will "find someone" and marry again. It is a required response and not truthful. What they are really thinking is if there is a way to haunt a new couple and make their lives miserable, I'm on it! Think about it. Do you really think they want a stranger redecorating and using their towels? Do you think they relish the idea of being replaced by a trophy wife or husband? Absolutely not! They secretly reserve the right to redecorate and find a trophy mate when their husband or wife pre-deceases them!

There really are things to fear, though.

Worry. Let's start there. Most of it centers on worrying about dying. Along with just about everything else. Will I outlive my money? Am I going to get sick? Will I have a painful death? Will I outlive my wife? Will my wife outlive me? Is there enough money to support her/him if I die? Would he/she marry him/her if I die first? There's plenty to worry about. And it increases as we age.

This one—flying—is personal. For some reason, I have suddenly become afraid of flying. I have flown tens of thousands of miles over most of the world. Now, I am reluctant to get on a plane.

I think 9/11 visuals have something to do with it, even though I have flown thousands of miles since. It may be the mysterious disappearance of a couple of planes in Asia. I cannot shake the horror of being in a plane that is plunging to the bottom of the ocean. Therapy time!

And there's even more serious stuff to worry about.

Who among us has not thought of the final chapter? Which is it going to be: cremation or traditional burial? This can get one going. I know people who are adamant about choosing cremation over the six feet under option. They can't stand the idea of being cooped up in a box for eternity. Somewhere in that rationale must be a concern that when they are buried, they will not actually be dead for eternity. It has happened. People have been buried alive, but as I understand it, doctors have recently gotten pretty good at determining when people are actually dead.

But, the idea of incineration is disturbing. At least for me. Anyone who has ever burned a finger knows that burns hurt. Add to this, the dilemma as to whether your loved ones are to bury a shoebox full of ashes in a traditional burial plot, or scatter the ashes in some favored place. I'm for scattering, primarily because I don't want to be cooped up in a box, big or little, for eternity.

Why do we even think about this? Really? After all, dead is dead. What I think it all seems to boil down to is that it is very difficult, even painful, for us to consider our death at all, much less what happens afterward.

To be realistic, there are other things that are probably more worrisome

For example, living alone. It is one thing to live alone. Another to be left alone. What a sad way to spend one's final days, months, or years. For some, living alone is a matter of choice. For many, it is the consequence of having lived too long and survived other meaningful people in their lives. For others, it can also be the consequence of having lived the kind of life in which people were inclined to leave you alone.

When I think of old people living alone, I'm reminded of a commercial about security devices in which an older woman says, "I've fallen and I can't get up." Not a good position to be in, literally or figuratively.

On top of that, what about falling? Older people do have a tendency to fall. It is a probable second only to a fear of serious illness or sudden death. There are probably statistics showing just how dangerous it can be in terms of mortality (see Mortality). People fall, and often become immobilized, develop hypostatic pneumonia, and, if they do pass, let's hope all the decisions for the immediate postmortem period have been made.

And speaking of falling, there's another aspect of falling that is troublesome. I refer to hair that falls out, teeth that fall out, arches that fall. Falling is going to get you one way or another. Then, of course, there's always falling out of favor with friends and relatives. (See Gravity)

What could be a source of greater fear and worry than fear of a stroke? There is no joy in being immobilized with a broken hip. But being immobilized by part of the brain shutting down, that causes an inability to move well—or at all—along with an inability to speak properly, or at all, is daunting.

Physical deterioration is a given as we age. Gravity takes its toll. Our muscles turn to mush, which, for some of us make it more and more difficult to open even the pill case. Our voices become softer and weaker as tired vocal cords stretch. That's the equivalent of turning down the volume. There's a word for that: presbyphonia. People have difficulty understanding what we say and become impatient while they repeatedly ask us to repeat ourselves. (See Losing Dignity)

Loss of eyesight and hearing is not uncommon as people age. Generally, it is a gradual process. (see Memory, Hearing, Eyesight) The degradation and eventual loss of these senses not only erode our independence, it steals such pleasures as reading and listening to music. Maybe even watching television or listening to the radio. Or partaking in meaningful conversation. As it's happening, it can be an excruciating acknowledgement of aging and recognition that things are getting worse physically.

Is it true, as some say, that loss of hearing is far more traumatic than loss of eyesight? That's a good subject for discussion … if these old vocal cords are up to it.

Of all of the things that older people fear or worry about, the loss of driving privileges may very close to the top. Of all the things cited here, losing independence is a critical milestone. Whether it's the need of a caregiver, the loss of key senses, the inability to go where one wants to go, when wants to go, the inability to drive puts the senior into a brand new realm. It's one that borders on isolation, and one from which they will never return. At the same time, one must worry about the ability of someone who has sight, hearing, and cognitive issues, to "compete" in routine or aggressive traffic situations. We've driven behind someone whose gray hair is barely visible above the driver's headrest, who is driving well below the speed of others, while straddling two lanes. Should they be driving?

That said, it helps to have siblings. When the time comes, having a brother or sister be the one to tell Mom or Dad, "I need the keys to your car … forever." This is most likely to happen about the time the kids have asked for the checkbook, saying they are more capable (a less than tacit implication that you are "incapable") of handling YOUR finances.

Finally, it's time to give up your fear of the microwave. Get one. They won't make you sterile. And, at our age, it doesn't matter anyway.

24: I Wish I Had ...

No life is perfectly lived. I doubt that no one can look back and not find those few seconds, moments, even much longer periods that could not have been better managed. Some are unavoidable. Some are life changing. Most could probably have been avoided. But, as we've all heard at one point or another, "Hindsight is 20-20."

Even so, some could have been avoided based on our choices. On that note, when we are younger, we often had the tendency to act on a whim. With time and maturity, and having the experience of living through those dumb choices, we hopefully make better choices and learn from our mistakes.

One particular "unavoidable" choice, and probably the most painful regret comes after the death of a friend or loved one. We look back on what wasn't said, what might—or should—have been said or done, but wasn't. And now can never be.

As the end nears, do you really want to say I wish I had:

- Spent more time with my family
- Told more people I care
- Had the courage to say what I thought in key situations
- Kept in touch with old friends
- Done the things I had always wanted to do but didn't have the courage, or wouldn't take the time to do them.
- Had the courage to leave that job I hated
- Taken more professional and personal risk
- Tried harder in school
- Exercised more and taken better care of myself
- Traveled when I had the chance
- Had managed my money better

Right now, if you are reading this, make a bucket list of people who do matter, and tell them. Take the time while you still have time.

Divorce, too, is a life choice that may or may not be regrettable. One might say, "I wish I'd tried harder to make it work." Or, "I wish I'd taken steps to end the misery earlier." For some, divorce could also rank high on a list of accomplishments. Even so, divorce is ranked right up there with the death of a child or a spouse in terms of traumatic events.

Sometimes some of the things we regret seem almost frivolous compared to those things we regret the most.

Nonetheless, they are regrets.

An older man can look back on youth with the sad realization that no fair young lass will ever flirt with him again. That young laughter and pranks are not happening again. The spontaneity of youth has long since given way to caution and worry. And so it goes. Regrets to be sure, but not of the category of a lost spouse or best friend.

There is sadness, too, in the discovery over time that there are fewer and fewer people who have the same life reference points as we do. It is on my list of regrets that as the present and the future overtake the past, there are fewer opportunities to reminisce, and fewer and fewer people with whom to share those life reference points.

How many people do you know who have ever heard *The Lone Ranger* on the radio, or remember collecting tinfoil for the World War II war effort, or who watched the Army-McCarthy hearings, or watched Milton Berle on television? There are now only a few people on the planet who remember my mother and father, and with whom I can reminisce about them. I regret that, and it makes me sad.

Not to mention the music of our time. Today's young people laugh at who we grew up listening to, from Tommy Dorsey and Frank Sinatra to Jo Stafford and the Four Aces. I suppose that gives us the right to comment from time to time about how outrageous today's popular music is. It is, isn't it? In time, these next generations will be

reminiscing and regretting their favorite songs are no
longer played.

There is a song entitled, "Yesterday When I Was Young,"
by Herbert Kretzmer and Charles Aznavour, and that
captures the essence of regret. The song has been performed
by many artists, though none capture it (at least to me) as
well as Aznavour's version. The lyrics are perfect poetry for
looking back over life's landscape when the view ahead is
short. He sings of how so many of us approach life in our
youth as a silly game, only to later regret the selfishness and
arrogance that left so many dreams unrealized. His words
capture the very bittersweet essence of regret. Fortunately,
his version is available online.

Listen to it.

You won't be sorry.

My own effort in reflecting on age, in poetry rather
than song, is not dissimilar.

Looking Back

I wake up each day thinking it may be the last
Few thoughts of the future, more of the past
A strange mix of people, places and things
Flash by in a blur including the flings

Names are forgotten, addresses long gone
East Orange and Vermont ... Munich and Bonn

Mistakes that were made, promises broken
Too many things ignored or unspoken

Regrets to be sure, and paths left untaken
People that mattered abandoned…forsaken
It's the tableau of a life not quite complete
Some things I would change, and others repeat

But it's too late for that, time's running out
The future's uncertain only shadows of doubt
What a gift it would be to re-live parts of the past
What's done is done…but, intact is the cast

That can't happen, of course, the record's engraved
Not much is left except memories saved
But they dim and they fade as if into thin air
Full clarity and detail are increasingly rare

All that's left is a future clearly uncertain
Moving full speed toward that final curtain
We don't have the chance to change things in the past
Regardless of the light in which they've been cast

It's time wasted to dwell on what's already been done
The past is the past, the tale's been spun
It's not like a page you can choose to erase
And to what would you do so if that were the case?

The future's the future whatever its length
Facing it boldly requires great strength
So don't go to bed tired and depressed
As if tomorrow will be some kind of test

The past is the past and can't be reversed
So, start living each day as if it's the first.
Your fate and your future await your arrival
The only obstacle left is, quite clearly, survival.

All the choices we make in life are based on what information we have at the time. There's a nifty book written by Chuck Klosterman in 2016 titled, *But What If We're Wrong?* It posits that what we believe today, as has been the case since we emerged from the muddy slime, is based on conditions, expertise, analysis, and even science of a former time. Much of it was accepted, until something new came along to challenge and contradict. He points out that the theory of gravity two thousand years ago was simple. If you dropped a rock, it fell to earth because that's where it felt it belonged. That was acceptable for fifteen centuries until Isaac Newton began to think about falling apples. Now, Newton's conclusions and the theory of gravity are being reexamined. So, it follows suit that today's certainties can, and often do, produce faulty thinking and conclusions, which can lead to bad decisions.

In short, Klosterman's point is, "We don't know what we don't know," and that what we now know, or think we know, will likely be overruled in time.

That's the kind of thing that can produce those annoying regrets.

25: Exercise

One cannot overestimate the importance of staying active. Nor can one underestimate the difficulty of pulling it off. Let's be clear: certain forms of exercise are definitely off the table at my age. I would definitely eliminate football, rugby, soccer, boxing, figure skating, kayaking, the triathlon, any rodeo events, lacrosse, gymnastics, whitewater rafting, racquetball and squash, vigorous tennis, ice skating, downhill skiing, cross country running, horseback riding, basketball, and backpacking. And ping pong.

Acceptable forms of exercise might include golf, however, the level of stress and frustration the game induces can actually be hazardous to your health. Remember, Bing Crosby died of a heart attack while playing golf. And for those who live close to a golf course, I hope your children don't take up the language they are likely to hear when a golfer shoots over par by, say, ten. Also, the expense of the game has risen to such a level that it can decimate your social security check. (See Parsimony)

Swimming can be acceptable, if limited to sitting along the edge of the pool and kick-splashing.

Bowling may have a place in your regimen if you perhaps limit the weight of your ball, or roll the ball with both hands after you bend over at the foul line. To keep the thing from strolling down the gutter, ask the manager to set up the gutter guards.

Shuffleboard is a retirement community standard.

Fishing. But I'm not a fisherman. For me, what could be more boring?

Walking is good for you, and there's nothing to learn with the possible exception of learning how to cross busy streets before lights change so as not to be caught dodging cars. It's best, by the way, to seek routes that include traffic islands. Just in case you can't hobble fast enough to cross the entire avenue.

See, it's not so bad after all.

Finding a nice neighborhood park for your walk is an added bonus. And, because your damn kids took your car keys from you, you have to walk to get there. So, you're getting exercise as you go to exercise. One thing I'd like to note here, though. Parks do have some drawbacks. Like an overabundance of geese. The beasts can turn hostile, especially during nesting season. And, they poop a lot—up to twenty-eight times every day. If you're counting, that's up to two pounds worth. So, you'll definitely want pay attention to where you're stepping. I've seen some walkers who are so preoccupied with high-stepping around the dollops, they walk into trees and lampposts. And no, I haven't ever done that. Yet.

Even more dangerous are bikers. It has been my experience that, unlike the signs that are plastered along busy streets and encourage motorists to "Share the Road," they do not like to share paths with walkers. In fact, I have been verbally abused by bikers who believe they have sole claim to any right of way. You'd think they were driving one of those big old Cadillacs or Lincolns from long ago. Plus, you cannot hear them coming. I've been nearly toppled as they whoosh up behind me, then flash by, often cursing. Too often, they don't take into consideration that you just may be totally preoccupied with dodging goose poop, and accidentally step into their path. Cyclists and goose poop be damned!

Another source of concern is owls. Yes, owls. Especially the Great Horned Owl. Forget the notion that they only come out at night. They are birds of prey with sharp talons very capable of destroying a swan, fox, or raccoon. I caution any walker not to wear fur caps while taking a winter woodland stroll. Remember, winter is a time of year when prey is scarce. One acquaintance tells the story of a late afternoon walk when he had the unnerving feeling that he was being watched. He was wearing one of those

Russian fur caps. He looked up and was dumbstruck to see an owl with an impressive wingspan gliding overhead, apparently sizing up that hat for attack.

I'd also advise walkers not to walk with small dogs in areas where owls dwell.

Maybe I should stick with sitting in a rocking chair for exercise. Push, glide. Push, glide. Seems a lot safer.

26: Nutrition For Old Folks

I'll have another slice of pizza please with a Big Mac on the side. Hold that. I'm only kidding.

Somewhat.

At our age, when it comes to eating, our nutritional choices tend to become more limited.

Pizza and burgers are still definitely something we older folks would like to order, but have been told by our kids and our doctors (who are overweight) not to eat like that. Ever! That makes me think of the little kid in *The Christmas Story* who wanted a Red Ryder BB gun, but was told no because it would put the kid's eye out. Did that happen? No! So, I doubt one slice of pizza with a Big Mac kicker will put me out of commission.

Maybe, maybe not. But who wants to take the chance. Cardiologists are, after all, pretty well educated in such matters although I suspect a few of them might sneak in a Big Mac from time to time.

Yes, I do realize the time comes when all the things we loved to eat growing up and into our earlier adulthood, eventually decide to stick around and become a permanent part of our midsections and bellies.

I like to point out to the nonagenarians approaching the century mark and proclaiming the secret to longevity to be a couple of stiff drinks every day, a lifetime of smoking, and lots of red meat, that I know people with that regimen who didn't make it to forty. But given the working definition of news, perhaps that's why the stories are deemed important enough to make the papers. I mean if the secret was defined as a lifetime of prayer, celibacy, and the Mediterranean Diet who would care? We'd much rather have confirmation that our bad habits aren't all that bad. And if we can document that they may actually be beneficial, that's a bonus happily seized.

Maybe that's why the alcohol and cigarette industries are still booming.

Alas, those of us who survived to middle age and beyond, in spite of countless grilled cheese sandwiches, hamburgers, and hot dogs, along with mountains of chips consumed in our youth, will have our day of reckoning. The Big Pharma has seen to that. They've scared us into believing that every case of indigestion is either acid reflux or a harbinger of cardiac arrest, and we find ourselves being ushered into the cardiologist's office by our children who just happen to be driving *our* car.

When that happens, life as we have known it is over. Which, on reflection, is better than life actually being over (see Mortality).

So, we follow the good doctor's advice. I call it "advice" but it is advice that sounds a lot more like a command. Or is it the other way around? Whatever. We reject the admonition at our mortal peril.

What follows is a life, or what remains of it, of dietary banishment of our favorite foods, like the Israelites wandering in the dessert for forty years. At least they got to eat bread. We have the promise of what? Milk and honey? Except for us, it should be 2 percent milk. But at least the glycemic index of honey works in our favor. Doing without for forty years is a little long. For some of us, two years is a stretch.

As older individuals, nutrition is a particular problem for us. It's a double-edged sword. One side involves what we can't eat; the other, what we can.

As kids we were told to eat everything. As baby boomers and children of depression-era and World War II parents, nothing was to be wasted. Plates were to be cleaned to a shine. "There are starving kids in China ...Eat!" Now, I suspect, however, it can be argued that many of the fast food industry franchises in China have helped to reduce China's population more than that country's one-child policy.

Eating became a big and important part of our culture. And, as kids we responded. We may have blanched at brussels sprouts. But, if we wanted to go out and catch lightening bugs after dinner, we ate them! The sprouts. Not the bugs. So eating was ingrained. And as we grew older, we happily obliged, especially when we had more control over what we ate.

We were privy to piecrusts made with lard. Fresh green beans cooked in fatback. Mayonnaise being left on a summer picnic table in the sun and people slathering it on sandwiches hours later, and never getting sick. Eating was good. Eating was fun. Eating was safe. If something didn't agree with us, we threw up and moved on.

So, there is a certain degree of culture shock when we are told what we cannot put on our plates. And, as we get older, there is no shortage of people who are perfectly comfortable telling us just that. Our doctors and our kids have it all figured out—or so they think. They seem especially fond of the bland. Hot spices are definitely out. And if you must eat that jalapeno, keep the Tums handy. Nothing containing a modicum of fat is allowed. Sugar's a no-no. Creamy sauces are to be avoided. Decaffeinated coffee only—if you must have coffee at all. And you probably should not. And nothing with white flour can be tolerated. We're encouraged to think soft foods: mashed potatoes, rice, pudding, almost any kind of puree are on the menu. Ensure. Pablum.

Oh, and stewed prunes.

For good reason.

They know what's good for our hearts, our stomachs, our eyesight, our teeth, and any other body part with any degree of functionality. Of course, the kids never broach the subject of any aphrodisiac. That would send them screaming from the room. Maybe that's not such a bad idea.

The menu might be long on content, but short on appetizing substance. Fish, whole grains, lots of greens. Olive oil is encouraged. Just look up Mediterranean Diet and that's pretty much it. It's not all that bad. Boring? Yes. Bad? No.

Hang on to those memories of southern fried chicken, prime rib, French fries, grits with gravy, cheese, eggs, salt, bacon, grilled food, processed food, sweets.

Oh, the hell with it. All I'm doing is making myself hungry.

So, our diets must change whether we like it or not. But I can't help but think of the fast food industry and how they continue to test our resolve in eating healthy.

As an invited speaker to the Centers for Disease Control (CDC) including scientists and agency leaders, harsh food critic of the US policies, Michael Pollan offered that Americans have an eating obsession. Of course he's been saying for years that that obsession involves eating the wrong things.

All in all, Pollan sums up what he'd learned about eating in seven simple words: "Eat food, not too much, mostly plants." One key word, here, I believe, is "plants".

Sure, the fast food places have added salads to their menu, but do they push those delectable delights on us? No. They push their burgers and fries and soft drinks. And to help us choose those delectable items, they SUPERSIZE them.

What's not to love about that? More belly fat—I mean, more bang—for your butt (this one was intentional).

In all of this, one thing is clear. We have to resist the industry's siren call to supersize anything, despite how attractive the pricing is to someone. Especially to those of us who are on a limited budget. Sadly, the actual cost can be measured in an obituary, as well as in obesity.

Regardless of what we eat, care should be taken at any age to eat something.

Now, after digesting all of this (pun very much intended), this brings me back to the Mediterranean Diet, which is touted to be good for us. Pizza was invented in Italy right? Does it not follow that pizza is good for us? Besides that, nutrition experts say to include five different, vibrant colors of veggies on the plate. Red is a color. Red is vibrant. Red is found in pizza. So, I think I will take that nice slice of pizza with a Big Mac kicker on the side. Yes, I know. I never said I was perfect.

27: Objection! Otherwise Known as Complaining, Whining, and What Have You

Where does one begin when it comes to complaining? Although complaining shows no boundaries with regard to age, it does seem to be part of the aging process. I think we've all heard some of the terms that are synonymous with older people: cranky, grumpy, cantankerous, crochety.

In very general terms, I believe the complaints come from the wellspring of pain and discomfort. People who feel good and who are in good humor tend to smile and laugh a lot. They tend to be more gregarious and forgiving. These are hardly qualities usually ascribed to the cantankerous and cranky.

The young may assume that older parents and grandparents are in some degree of pain or discomfort just about all of the time. If you doubt me, just listen for what are uncharitably called, "old people sounds."—grunts, groans, wails, yelps, whimpers, howls, and sighs, as well as other sounds for which there is no particular category. Other words, like Ouch! Damn! Ugh! Ooh! work quite well, too.

Any or all can emote accordingly as the result of any form of exertion, like getting out of their favorite chair to sit down at the kitchen table, bending over to pick up something, or when standing back up after bending over to pick something up.

The noises can even be heard after no exertion at all. It can be a loud sigh when contemplating some form of exertion. Like having to get up out of the chair. This sigh ratchets up a notch when there is a suggestion to do something they do not want to do, like exercise. Gramps or Nana use this auditory clue for another reason, too. To lay on the guilt, which sometimes will work and the unwelcome suggestion will thereby be withdrawn. Other times, though, the noise is just considered another "old person sound" and disregarded altogether.

It should be noted here, that more often than not, the negative reaction to come along for a short road trip, to say the market, is not because the older person does not want to go where they are being invited. It's usually because it involves some form of exertion, such as having to get up from their chair, walk to the car, get into the car, get out of the car, get back in the car, get out of the car, and sit back down in their chair. Just thinking about this makes me groan.

One that can be expected to inspire a crisp yelp, moan groan, or an outright howl, is gout. Gout was once thought to be a problem limited to royalty and the wealthy; those people prosperous enough to eat and drink too well. Actually, it is caused by a collection of uric acid crystals. Very commonly a problem that presents in the big toe, which makes putting on a shoe a huge ordeal. Characterized by redness, stiffness, swelling, heat, and pain, even the weight of a bed sheet can be excruciating. This pain is severe and worthy of numerous "old people sounds," like, "Damn! Crap! Oh, no!" They are usually expressed at some volume.

Another source of common complaining amongst the elderly—and that can affect someone at any age—is arthritis. (Gout is a type of arthritis.) I learned there are about one hundred types of this degenerative disease. None of them good. Not only can the pain be debilitating, it can sometimes lead to disfigurement. I have it in my fingers, I'm sure the result of pounding a manual typewriter for forty years or so. I also have it in other various joints. I'm sure it's the result of the number one cause of arthritis. Aging!

Then there's this: Indigestion. It can come at any age. Even children may have issues, and they were dealt with quickly and with dispatch. We threw up. Often on our parents. The most clever of us learned to escape punishment by feigning pain—stomach or otherwise. Sympathy goes a long way when a parent thinks their kid is ill. Unfortunately, much later in life, pain is no longer feigned.

Like in the teenage years, for instance, things were quite different. Teens can eat just about anything, and often do. They rarely get sick as a result. But, if and when they do, it is not a spectacle any adult ... or anyone for that matter ... would wish to behold. As drinking seems to be a right of passage in some teens, indigestion and worse often comes from having imbibed too freely. Often this happens after eating too much pizza, hot dogs, or nachos and cheese. The very unpleasant side effect of barfing is just as painful for the witnesses of the event as for the afflicted. God forbid the kid tries the once-cute trick of throwing up on Mom or Dad. It was never really cute in a toddler....and much less so in a teen.

Acid reflux is yet another related digestive issue. Who ever heard of it twenty, thirty, forty years ago, when everything going on in the gastrointestinal grid was diagnosed as indigestion or heartburn? Now that Big Pharma has elbowed its way into our lives on television and the evening news, it is part of our everyday conversation. Every time we burp, we self-diagnose, and the diagnosis is acid reflux. If it is, it's treatable. If it's not, it can be more serious than even the commercials would imply.

The basic problem with gastrointestinal problems may not be with the individual issues themselves. What any oldster who is aware thinks just about every time there is a twitch or hitch between the tonsil and the stomach is the possibility that he or she is having a heart attack, or that cancer is destroying the throat, esophagus, or larynx. There's a big difference between Tums as a treatment and radiation therapy or bypass surgery. That's more of a concern, or should be, than heartburn or a simple case of too much salsa. Lingering problems of this sort, as we all know, should be put before a medical professional post haste.

My father had a sore throat for a week or two before he went to a doctor. Men (and perhaps increasingly, some women) too often delay seeking treatment. Unfortunately, within twenty-four hours of seeing the doctor, he was on the operating table having his larynx removed.

He never spoke normally again. He made funny, not funny in the usual sense, but unusual and guttural word-like sounds by squeezing what he called a controlled burp through what was left of his throat. By the way, for most of his adult life, he smoked up to four packs of unfiltered Old Gold cigarettes a day. It was a hell of a way to quit smoking. Because he could no longer draw breath through his throat. He breathed through a hole in his chest the size of a quarter. His smoking days were over.

An interesting note here. Dad spent several weeks in group therapy learning how to control that burp and make words. I was shocked to learn that during breaks, fellow laryngectomy patients went outside to smoke. They had found a way to hold the cigarette to that hole near their neck and inhale through it. This image definitely puts a new spin on the power of the addiction to nicotine.

Another complaint, and oftentimes, the butt of jokes: Constipation. Honestly, though, it can become a serious medical issue. Best cure for that is prune juice. Until relief occurs, many may suffer in silence. Who wants to have to explain what's going on? Certainly not me. I'd rather suffer in silence. Food for thought to the younger set: When you attach an adjective to Gramps or Gram like grumpy or cranky, think constipation. Another thing to keep in mind. When the problem is resolved, silence is usually not an option.

The aches and pains, twitches and twinges we all experience are usually not the first vestiges of heart failure, stroke, cancer, or diabetes. Chances are overwhelming that as we age, we'll experience them all.   Aches and pains, although part of life, are a definitive part of aging. But, considering the alternative, I'll go with it.

28: Things to Avoid

One of the sure signs of aging is the realization that the list of things you find yourself avoiding grows a lot longer. I'm not anti-social, but I now prefer smaller groups and gatherings to larger ones. My maximum is about two. With me being one of the two.

High school or college class reunions are no longer high on my list of social activities. Especially after the fortieth or fiftieth. There are myriad reasons. First and foremost, they remind me of my age. It is discouraging to see the prom king and queen; the football star or cheerleader captain, ten, twenty, or thirty years after their prime. They look nothing as they did. Most are overweight. Then there are the wrinkles and the thinning or absent hair, all of which remind us of our own *avoirdupois* and thinning skin. Somehow, class nerds who were non-descript and relegated to second class citizenship at the old alma mater, come out of it a lot better over time than the kings and queens of campus, as everyone probably knew they would right from the start.

There is also the showmanship. Or should I say the show-one-up-manship. Those first few reunions are either unbearable, or wildly entertaining as the various classmates (in this phase, I call them "cast members") work hard at trying to impress with alleged success. It is a bona fide competition, and only ends after the thirty or fortieth reunion. That's when people have finally become resigned—or have accepted—whatever they are, or with whatever they have, or don't have.

But, there's a downside. The longer the interval between graduation and the reunion, the more depressing it becomes. The attendees may be more honest and content with themselves in the later years, but there are fewer of them. It's another sign that time is marching on without many of us, and that we're marching along with it. Overweight, humped over, or balding we may be resigned to what we have, or have not become, but that doesn't mean we aren't frustrated and even resentful with where our journey through life took us. So, for me, I find it best to forego the reunions and keep in touch via Facebook, where one can lie with abandon, and it doesn't matter if you do it with a straight face or not.

And then there's nursing homes. I can just bet that for anyone reading this, when I say, "Old people smell," nursing homes tend to come to mind. The combination of urine, lilac, wet flannel, cheap aftershave, toilet water, and old slippers, with a generous wafting of various medications and food are nauseous. Add to this the general landscape of residents sitting in corners with blank stares being attended—or not attended to—by often indifferent, underpaid, and overworked staff, and the homes become even more depressing.

Maybe this is why people avoid visiting loved ones. Is it our out of sight, out of mind tendency to ignore something that is painful to see, or to deal with for that matter? Or are do they become invisible, non-existent, because we can't bear to think that may be us one day?

In all fairness, family members may, for any number of reasons, sometimes feel guilty for having put their loved one in a nursing home. Some are angry over what it's costing them to have auntie housed there, or frustrated they don't have the wherewithal to house them in a better place. Maybe they are angry at themselves because they aren't able to take care of Mom, or Dad, or Grandmother by themselves. Sometimes, it could be because relatives don't want the challenge or obligation to care for a parent. Or that they had been caring for them before putting them into a home because they'd had enough. Sad, but true.

I have been to nursing homes and was told by caregivers that some residents are never, repeat *never*, visited by anyone, including the sons or daughters who had them admitted in the first place. Not even by nieces or nephews or those adorable grandkids.

For the most part nursing homes can be terrifically depressing places to visit. It's hard to imagine actually living there 24/7. I'm sure many of us as we've grown older think about what our own kids would do if that time came. Would they choose a nursing home over reciprocating the care we gave them when they weren't able to care for themselves. We all hope they'd choose the later, I imagine.

Of course, now, to make the idea of having to move from one's life-long home and independence, the term "Assisted Living" has become the more palatable term. Or moving to an independent living community.

In either case, bring your money belt to both.

While we may not avoid nursing homes forever, here are a few things we should definitely avoid:

- Buying a computer or tablet or smartphone late in life. It's a bad idea unless you want to be dependent on a 13 year old.
- Wearing Bermuda shorts with long black socks and tennis shoes. It is not a good look, period!
- Wearing Bermuda shorts with long black socks and sandals. It's an even worse look.
- Wearing white socks with everything else. Why do we do it?
- Ski trips. Unless the only reason you go is to drink hot toddys by the fireplace.

- Roller skating
- Entering a triathlon.
- Taking up smoking
- Visiting relatives for extended periods of time.
- Sad movies. Why do we get weepy as we get older?
- Thinking we can do the things we did at age forty. No matter what you think, we can't. That would include staying up late, working long days, exercising vigorously, having vigorous (or any kind of) sex, buying a new house, horseback riding, skiing, and just about any other sport. And, of course, sex. Did I mention that? Therefore, making a reservation for a week at Club Med is probably not a good idea.

Things we can do (and probably should):

- Cataract surgery
- Go to bed early
- Sleep in
- Visits with grandkids (short)
- Medical checkups
- Make a will
- Study probate laws and procedures
- And, come to think of it, vacation at Club Med. Why not? It's all inclusive.

29: Parsimony

Is there ever a time in our lives in which we are not worried about, or somehow fixated on, money? Maybe between the ages of birth to five years old. After that, it affects the rest of our lives. First, we worry about our allowance. Then we worry about getting a part-time, minimum wage job to earn a few bucks. It's never enough. Then it's paying for our first car, college debt, which is, increasingly, something close to a lifetime obligation. Then careers, salaries, a new home, spouse, or baby. Never mind, our grown-up toys. And of course, now, for us oldsters, retirement. Did we buy enough life insurance for our surviving spouse? Were our investments (if we were lucky enough to have some) enough? Will we live long enough to enjoy what we worked for all our lives? Or will there be enough to sustain us until we are done?

No wonder we become increasingly parsimonious as we age. We have no idea what the answer to any of the questions will be, or how circumstances will change to impact our financial situation.

For our purposes here, we can skip the concerns we'll have up to the time we are post-career. That will all play out as it will. It's how it plays out at the end that is our concern. Keep in mind that we've spent a lifetime worrying about money. If you are independently wealthy, you may feel that you can stop reading right here. You can. But five will get you ten (as if you need it since you're rich) that you still have some concerns about money. You probably worry about keeping what you have! (See Scams)

That's the concern for the rest of us, too. Part of our problem that we, at least most of us, are living on fixed incomes. Income is the same month after month. We do not have the opportunity to add to it, unless we go back to work, or Uncle Sam gives us a Social Security cost of living increase, or unless our 401k gets a little kick from a growing stock market. Or unless some long-forgotten aunt or uncle leaves us a lot of money. Or even a little money.

On the other hand, things can go the other way, as when our 401k takes a hit when the market drops. Or when the company we worked for so long goes belly up, taking all former employees' pension money with it.

A word to the wise here. If you're under forty and reading this, get in on whatever savings plan, 401k, pension alternative your employer offers. If none is available, start putting money away on a sustained basis to build a retirement account. It's best to have the money automatically deducted from your salary or your checking account. That way, you don't miss it. Plus, it adds up more quickly than you think, and will be an invaluable addition to retirement income. If you haven't started. Do it today. Tomorrow, aka, retirement will be here sooner than you can imagine. Social Security may not be here at all. It could suddenly go away. How long have we been hearing that it is only a matter of time before it goes belly up? Many say the government won't let that happen. I certainly hope not. But I'd still keep an eye out.

Think about it. If you're in your forties, that gives you another twenty-five years or so to accumulate funds for retirement. This day and time, thanks to modern medicine, you will likely live more than twenty years after you stop working. Keep your fingers crossed that whatever instrument or account you placed your money in maintains a healthy and steady growth. It's best to spend a few bucks and consult with a financial advisor and/or tax advisor.

End of lecture.

Why mention all of this? Well, retired people are many times perceived as cheap, stingy, or parsimonious. The better word here is "careful." Mindful of the many things that can go wrong financially, older people worry that what they've worked and saved all of their lives for is in constant jeopardy. The stock market can swoon and does periodically. How many non-housing bubbles are out there?

Plus, there's always concern about catastrophic illness. Even with Medicare, supplementary Medicare insurance, and the Affordable Care Act, the financial hit can be extreme. God forbid if there's no medical insurance. A prolonged hospital stay, whether it be for complicated surgery or treatment can wipe out six or seven figures in savings very, very quickly. Snap, it's gone.

There's always the fear of outliving whatever money we've managed to stash away. It's a given that we all want to live a long, healthy life. Many of us are living, or will live that longer life. That, along with not having enough for a surviving spouse to live in comfort, is enough to turn a guy's hair gray. If he has any hair, in which case, his head may just turn red. And, as we know, when it comes to money, red is not a good color.

There's also a psychological reason for keeping one hand on the wallet or purse. The depression. I'm not talking about a "downturn," or even a three- or four-year recession. I'm talking about the big one. The Grand Kahuna. The one that ravaged the thirties. Our parents lived through the Great Depression. They learned from it, and they passed on what they learned to us. The lessons were to save for that rainy day (or decade), spend wisely, stay out of debt, do what you can yourself, live simply rather than lavishly, and don't waste anything. On the one hand that's a boon to those of us who remember those times. For those who don't and who have grown up in times of prosperity, I don't always see this mindset. Live for today seems to be something of a mantra.

Hopefully the foregoing will help our kids and others who may be the ones taking care of us in the future remember our parsimony. Our tendency to be tight with a buck. That's why my friends play golf on the weekdays rather than weekends. The green fees are not as high. It's why so many shop at discount grocers and outlet malls. It's why they clip coupons and scour the paper (if they subscribe to one) for bargains. It's why men wait a few extra days or weeks before getting haircuts. It's why, when they go out to eat, they look for the closest happy hours. It's why so many seniors frequent thrift shops. Lots of bargains there. Who needs new stuff? The problem is the items you like probably belonged to someone who died.

Whatever the opportunity to save money might be, they're on it. And most of them are pretty darn good at sniffing out bargains.

In other words, our parsimony and saving money is a mission. Except, of course, when it comes to buying gifts for the grandkids.

30: Napping

We are told that the great men of history, and I presume women, all napped. Winston Churchill, JFK (who may or may not have napped alone), Cleopatra, and Catherine the Great. Actually, I don't know about the last two. I made that up in order to remain gender inclusive. What more incentive does one need to take an afternoon snooze than to look at the greats of history who napped. Go to your happy place for a quick nap as a dolt, and wake up as a candidate for president. How else would you explain the quality of our politicians. They must all nap! Come to think of it … not all.

Perhaps only one or two.

Today, perhaps none.

Now, it's important to distinguish the difference between napping and dozing. To doze is also a reference to falling asleep. The difference being that a nap is planned. One decides to take a nap. Not so with dozing. That's unplanned. One might doze while watching television, or listening to a wife talking about her latest shoe purchase. The wife might doze while her husband explains the ground rule double or infield fly rule. A word to the wise: dozing under either of these circumstances can be harmful to relationships.

In researching the subject of napping, I discovered that many non-nappers' view of napping is neither flattering nor accurate. Critics believe people who nap are either old or lazy, and that nappers lack ambition and have low standards. Talk about piling on the stereotype.

Given this misimpression, I suggest you may want to keep your naps secret. If you must tell people you nap, tell them that you take a "power" nap. It's not exactly certain what a power nap is, but the word "power" does seem to suggest a positive. You are not weak. You are not passive. You are powerful! You close your eyes while you plug in and recharge! Let them make fun of you at their peril.

Actually, research tells us about one in three Americans nap, and that more men do than women. Research also shows that daily naps of ten to forty minutes are very good for the practitioner. It shows that they usually waken with more energy and drive, and that they are more alert. Now that's more like it.

In spite of this positive research, older people seem reluctant to take that afternoon nap. I have heard of some who nap feel absolutely horrible afterward. Bearish, even.

Another reason might be that they are afraid that they will have trouble getting to sleep at night. That can happen.

Another reason an older person might pass on the nap is a condition that often surfaces even during short, afternoon naps. Drooling! Drooling is a phenomenon that does not always present itself during the normal nighttime slumber, though at times, I've been known to wipe the slobber from my mouth.

Afternoons? That's a different story.

For whatever reason, many people have a tendency to drool while napping. There is a possible explanation in the research. Apparently, there is a slight relaxation of the muscles during the light sleep that is typical of a brief nap, although researchers don't disclose exactly what muscles are involved. It might be instructive to find out how to exercise them so they stay firm and taut. We don't want them relaxing when we're awake or at dinner. Or while making a presentation, or even while playing checkers at the fire station.

There is also something called "sleep inertia." Some people who go into a deep sleep, even for a short period of time, may wake up feeling both disoriented and fuzzy...or groggy. It may take several minutes for this to pass. There can be a period of confusion. In other words, it's a lot like getting up in the morning. To alleviate that grogginess, my best advice for those suffering from sleep inertia is to take another nap.

Again, the experts tell us that the best naps are those that are taken in the napper's own bed, and in a darkened, quiet room with a comfortable room temperature. To me, that makes sense anytime.

Other places in which the would-be napper is comfortable will also work. Here I'm thinking sofa or easy chair. We definitely want to avoid drifting off while driving, or in the barber chair. Given a choice of the two, take the chair. Better to wake up with a bad haircut than to have a potentially fatal accident.

For those of you who think successful napping is automatic, it's not. Like other activities or exercises you'd like to master, it takes some practice. Aside from finding a comfortable and familiar place to nap, the napper must determine the right time of day to indulge. Afternoon's are definitely best. But pulling up the covers too late in the afternoon will likely affect the ability to go to sleep at the normal bedtime.

There are some would-be nappers who decline to hit the sack because they don't want to wonder what their spouse was doing during their absence. Or this could merely become a concern of young people with attractive wives or husbands.

Like babies are known to do, some older people fight the urge to nap for fear they might miss something while sleeping. That's probably unlikely at this point in our lives, since so little happens when we're awake.

Some don't want to nap for fear that suggesting their spouse join them might be misconstrued as a romantic overture when really all they want to do is nap.

Still others don't want to nap because they're afraid they won't wake up at all.

31: Seniority and the Baggage That Comes With It

Seniority, if I may use the term, does not necessarily refer to a certain age. In fact, there have been lively discussions about the term itself, and when it applies to a particular situation or person. Various surveys seem to indicate that the designation varies from person to person, and that, no surprise here, it varies pretty much according to age. In other words, people who are younger will say old age begins at a younger age, whereas older people say it begins at an older age. For instance, a 30 year old might say old age begins at 60. A 50 year old might choose 75.

There is an oft-quoted adage that says, "To me, old age is always fifteen years older than I am." Not bad. In fact, it's good enough to be attributed to Bernard Baruch, Francis Bacon, John Burroughs, and Thomas Bailey Aldrich, just to name a few. Notice the reference is to "old age" and not to senior or senior citizen.

Before we move on, let's all agree on avoiding the term

"golden years." There's nothing golden about them. The phrase makes getting older sound like a fairy tale rather than the hard reality it is, and it ignores all the baggage that goes with it.

It seems the world cannot agree on how to classify older people, or even when that classification should be applied. Is it when we receive that first contact from the AARP at age 50? Is it when we retire? Is it when we are first offered a "senior discount?" That one is particularly hard to parse because senior discounts begin at age 50 in some cases, 55 in others, 60 in others. These are practically whippersnapper ages in my book.

The fact they are called "senior" discounts tends to tilt the discussion toward the word "senior." One British study says old age begins at age 80. That is also an age at which a great many people are dead.

Others prefer other designations such as:
- Elderly
- Elder
- Old people
- Oldsters
- Seniors
- Senior citizens
- Aged
- Retiree
- Aging seniors (What is this? Some kind of sub-category?)

Definitely on the unacceptable list:
- Over the hill
- Old coot
- Dirty old man
- Little old lady (sometimes little old lady in tennis shoes)
- Hag
- Crone

So, the answer as to when someone becomes any of the above is hardly fixed in stone. Perhaps the more important question is when does anyone feel that they have attained "senior," "elder," or "oldster," or even "old coot" status? It does not appear there is a moment, or even a day or year in which any of us feel we've "arrived" or crossed the threshold from middle age to old age.

In fact, there is also a debate as to when middle age begins. Presumably similar rules apply; the younger you are, the earlier you will say middle age begins. And like those of us who pinpoint old age much later than the younger set, the middle-aged individual considers middle age considerably later than a younger person. I guess Einstein was right. Everything's relative.

There is a real problem when it comes to the issue of age-guessing game. It is fraught with danger for anyone assuming someone is older than they are. Indulge me as I take on the subject in my 2010 book titled *How To Be Rude Politely* (from (Reedy Press, St. Louis, MO. 2010).

WHEN SOMEONE ASKS YOU
TO GUESS THEIR AGE

This can be very tricky, and requires an absolute ability to fib with alacrity. There are some very basic rules to remember, and woe be the one who confuses these rules.

You must remember that women like to be told they seem younger.

Men like to be told they are in terrific shape for whatever age they are

(Always guess low).

Old people like to tell you their age, so generally no guessing is involved.

You must follow by telling them they look like they have the energy and vigor of someone years younger.

Boys up to age 18 or 19 like to be told they look older than they are (This

is generally so they can feel they can buy beer without being detected).

Girls up to age 18 like to be told they look up to four or five years older.

After age 21, they must always be told they look younger

So, there is no trick to it. Compliments, graciousness, diplomacy. No problem. However, this chapter is titled what to do "When Someone Asks You to Guess Their Age." This puts a whole new wrinkle on the problem.

To begin with, it is inherently unfair for anyone to put another human being in this position. If the privilege is to be granted at all, it should be only to small children. It is a right they should lose automatically at age 13.

Nonetheless, there are those who ask it. Vanity is generally the motive. It creates an entire body of discipline. You must resist the temptation to tell the truth.

Who among us hasn't had the urge, when asked by a middle aged woman to guess her age, to respond by saying something like, "With or without makeup?"

How many times has an older man or woman asked, "How old do you think I am." You want to respond by saying, "Old enough to have the world's worst breath, and more liver spots than a kid with measles."

When a 14 year old boy poses the question, which is rare, you have to rein in the comment, "Not old enough to have grown into your nose yet."

And, the teen princess wants to hear something flattering about her face or form. Don't ever say, "Obviously, you're quite a young lady, just not old enough to have tits."

As for the middle aged man who challenges your honesty, it is difficult to resist the temptation say, "You look pretty good, with the legs and face of a man half your age, and the belly of one twice as old."

Alas, we can't say what we want, even when we're asked to play the guessing game. And, there is danger here. The danger is the possibility, and in some cases, the probability of guessing too high. You must always remember that the question is being asked because the person asking it does not believe he or she looks his or her age. They're proud of it. If you guess too high, in the case of all women and most men, or too low in the case of most seniors, you have been coerced into an insult.

Insults are something we like to avoid on most occasions. Although there are ways of doing it without the person on the receiving end realizing it.

We can dispose of the senior first. Your response should be, "I don't know how old you are, but you look better than I do." It will be greeted with some disappointment, but better safe than sorry.

To the middle age man, try something like, "I don't know, but you still look like you could go ten rounds with Julia Roberts." He'll like that. Come to think of it, the older guy might like it too.

Now, for the woman who asks. Women never ask such a question until they are in their forties, fifties or older. Younger women don't dare risk the chance of being told they look older than they are. The older women are usually desperate to be told they look younger. Men too, for that matter, though they like that notion that no matter what, their virility is unquestioned.

For starters, you can tell the woman that she looks like she could still go ten rounds with Brad Pitt. If they don't blush, answer 40. If they do, say 29.

As a matter of fact, 40 is a pretty good age for most women who would ask the question. My experience tells me that the question is most often asked by women between the ages of 43 and 57. So, 40 will usually work very nicely.

There may be a time when a woman will ask you to guess her age, and using my formula, you guess 29. If she tells you she's really 50, THEN tell her she looks like she could go ten rounds with you. After your answer, she probably will.

Real laugh lines can come from discussions of age and aging. Someone once said, "You are only as old as you feel." It has been said tens of millions of times since it was first uttered. And, it was probably the work of a 30 year old at that. What does it mean? I "feel" like I can do a lot of things. And I certainly want to do a lot of things. But

I can't because of physical limitations that are the direct result of being older, arthritic, and on medication.

"Never felt better in my life." Anyone over fifty who says that is trying to fool you, or themselves. Show me a man or woman who feels better at 50, 60, or 70 than when they were much younger, and I'll show you someone who forgets what it was like to be 15 or 20 or 25.

"Sex gets better in middle age." It may get better, but it also is less frequent, so it's pretty much of a wash.

"I would not want to be getting out of college or looking for my first job today." That may depend on the age of the person uttering these words. If our narrator is forty and in the middle of a good career, that may be true. If those words are spoken by a septuagenarian, it is BS pure and simple. What they really should be saying is, "I'd give up my Lipitor in a heartbeat if I could return to my high school years."

In terms of fixing the time when one can feel certain that old age has arrived, it seems to make sense that individuals determine it themselves. One way might be to use the contents of this book. If you are increasingly aware of your own mortality, make old people sounds, blanch when you see yourself in a full-length mirror, have issues with memory, hearing, or eyesight, and are always cold, chances are you are have either attained old age, or are bordering on it. If you wear over-the-calf black socks with Bermuda shorts and smell vaguely of something kinda-stale, sorta-medicinal, and sorta-uriney, well, that's a dead giveaway you are an "oldster" and quite possibly an "old coot" to boot.

32: Grandparents

Let me begin with one of my undeniable realities. All babies, when they are born, no matter their heritage, and for some time thereafter, resemble one or more of the following: Winston Churchill, Nikita Khrushchev, Edward G. Robinson, Hattie McDaniel, Gary Coleman, Mao Tse-tung, or Kim Jong-Un. Regardless, to grandparents those young'uns are more beautiful than life. Yup, even Kim Jong-Un was a welcome arrival, though to many, his departure would be even more so.

It is one of the laws of nature that something happens when we become grandparents. I can say this even though I am not one. Many older people tend to resist wanting to become grandparents because it is just another confirmation that they are old. But others cannot wait for their children to bear children and even begin to lobby for it before the engagement ring is sized. And, this is where the trouble can, and often does, begin.

There is a very strong tendency on the part of grandparents-to-be, and when grandparenthood actually arrives, to take over. Well, if not take over, to simply stage manage. (I'll have more on that in a bit.)

And, when said grandchild arrives, grandparents, whatever their predilection beforehand, become totally transformed into doting beings of love and affection. There are few, if any, exceptions to this. The lives of grandparents become totally dedicated to the newcomer, and that rarely ever changes. While there is still some truth to the old saying that the "nice thing about being a grandparent is that the children go home to their parents when the visit's over." There may be something to that, but the number of visits is the important part. And that number is usually high, whether it's a visit by the grandchild/grandchildren to the grandparents or vice versa.

I actually have a friend who regularly travels to the Netherlands to babysit the grandkids. Others have been known to move to be closer to the kids. My own brother-in-law is yet another case in point. His personality is one that might charitably be described as gruff. His tolerance level for the mundane has always been low. He looked forward to retirement. Then the grandkids started coming. That's when he started going. Going as in making daily trips to the grandkids' home to babysit. It is no small feat. The trip is forty miles each way. He does it daily, and revels in dressing, feeding, and bathing three kids, including twins under the age of three. He has been totally transformed and can change a diaper lickety-split.

CBS correspondent Leslie Stahl was so enthralled about becoming a grandmother she wrote a book about it. *Becoming Grandma.*

What is remarkable about it is, as she writes, that her first grandchild, and later a second, have become the most important thing that has ever happened to her. This even supersedes her professional role as a journalist in which she has covered some of the most important news events of a generation. She gushes in her effusiveness over the kids. She routinely travels from her home in New York to visit them in California. And when she can't, she is in constant touch via social media and Skype.

She wrote about it because, as a good journalist, she wanted to find out why she and other grandparents react as they do. Among her findings is the research that shows the hormonal and chemical reaction to a grandchild is the same cocktail that's unleashed when men and women fall in love. She adds that there is a "purity" in the emotion of that love, and that it defines "joy."

She cites anecdotal evidence that grandchildren can be therapeutic and even curative. Her husband's Parkinson's Disease symptoms were reduced when the grandkids were around. Her late colleague Bob Simon suffered from depression, but the arrival of the first grandchild seemed at least a partial, if not complete cure.

Grandparents are themselves, she writes, transformed to the point where their own children don't recognize them. They are no longer the policemen they were with their own children, but rather playmates to the grandkids.

She points to foster grandparent programs that have proved extremely beneficial to everyone involved.

Leslie Stahl's personal experience is, of course, her own. But her research includes some cautionary advice for grandparents and grandparents-to-be that is corroborated by many other grandparents. Some of them have learned it the hard way.

She writes that "not speaking your mind is the first commandment of grandparenthood." There is a sometimes irresistible temptation to become overly involved. I mentioned above that stage management can begin long before a baby is conceived. There's the push to "give me a grandchild." There can be pressure to get involved in naming the baby, "suggesting" in what religion a child should be raised if parents are of different religions. The "advice" can cover every contingency and can generate significant friction.

Grandparents are advised not to compete with their counterparts, i.e., the "other" grandparents. Competing mothers-in-law can generate Category 4 consequences. At times these storms can cause a break in the relationship between grandparents, parents, and in-laws. According to Ms. Stahl, this can be tragic, because it can keep the grandparents from seeing, or even being allowed to see the grandchildren. She ends with an appeal to parents and grandparents not to let this happen, not to ever let anything come between the lives of children and their grandparents.

The kids, she reminds us, will be the worse off for it, as will the grandparents. Even if the child looks like Edward G. Robinson, Gary Coleman or … shudder … Kim Jong-Un.

33: Social Isolation

Social isolation, living alone, and loneliness are far too common a problem in the world of the elderly. It happens when a spouse dies, the children, if there are any, are in another part of the country, or if you've been a bitch or bastard and no one wants to be with you. Sometimes it's all three. It can also occur when body odor reaches critical mass. We'll let that one speak for itself and move on.

Sometimes it also happens by choice.

It's difficult to imagine being alone when the number of older people is growing so rapidly. Dr. John Morley, the Director of the Division of Geriatric Medicine at the Saint Louis University School of Medicine refers to a geriatric "tsunami." The number of people sixty-five and older is expected to triple by the middle of this century. That will be one-and-a-half-billion seniors on the planet. It is also estimated that in fifteen years, one in five Americans will be sixty-five or older. It hardly sounds like a prescription for loneliness. But loneliness is an issue with many older people.

Every senior dreads the, "I've fallen and I can't get up" scenario. That's the number one fear of being alone. The prospect of a disabling accident or sickness with no one immediately available to help, and no means of communicating the problem, is probably assisted living's most effective promotional tool. There are other concerns as well.

There are many aspects of loneliness and even many phases. You can be alone and not lonely. You can be with people and feel lonely when you feel you are not connecting and realize that when the people are gone, you will be alone and feeling psychologically isolated. The connection with the rest of humanity is gone. With that can come a desperate loneliness borne of a feeling of being unworthy, unloved, or unaccepted. All of which is apparently what Mother Teresa was referring to when she spoke of "the poverty of loneliness."

It is also possible to feel alone even when you are not. You can be with someone and still be lonely. It suggests a bad relationship or an inability or unwillingness to connect. Professionals will encourage anyone in this circumstance to, as the old telephone company ad encouraged, "reach out and touch someone." I'm suggesting something beyond making a phone call. Go where people are. Join a club. Find a way to interact.

That might include getting a dog or a cat. Just having something to care for in return for unconditional love can be extraordinarily helpful. On second thought, if you want a pet's unconditional love, forget the cat. Stick with the dog.

If one's isolation is the result of BO, you can always blame that particular ambiance on the dog or the kitty litter. Kitty litter is the most effective means of shifting blame. However, with kitty litter, the downside is that there is usually a cat that goes along with it. And that you eventually have to empty the litter box.

By the same token, one can be alone but not be lonely. Some people enjoy being alone and are alone by choice. Indeed many of us seek out times when we can be alone with our thoughts or our hobbies. It is when it is not by choice and when there is little prospect of not being alone, that depression can be overwhelming. That creates its own set of issues.

Science is beginning to determine that loneliness can lead to early death. Resulting depression causes people to lose interest in properly caring for themselves and can encourage important behavioral changes. They eat and sleep poorly. They may take important medications erratically. They may just stop caring.

Loneliness can also be fleeting. It can be crushing during holidays or important anniversaries. Memories of missing loved ones and happy times are often triggered by a holiday. Especially sad for many people is the anniversary of the death of a loved one. It is usually a date that is engraved in memory, and like a cruel psychological annuity, the loneliness and realization return year after year before, during, and after the anniversary date. These periods are a good time to work at not being alone. However, it must be noted, one can never escape the calendar.

34: Resistance to Change

The gene that guides us to embrace new things when we are younger must mutate slowly as we age. As teens, and young men and women, we loved to try new things. Dare I say that it helped us mature. We were impatient to find new worlds, whether they be across the street or across the ocean; whether it be new fads, new foods, or new friends, we could go with it. We were invigorated by change and welcomed new impulses that got the adrenaline going and the blood pumping. It was part of the process of growing up. In short, an early step in the process of aging, although we would never have thought of it in that way at that time.

Some psychologists and behaviorists have explanations for the resistance to change as we age. I almost referred to it as a fear, but it's probably too strong a word. Some of the reasons cited include:

Loss of control. There's concern that whatever is changing puts you behind the curve and having to hustle to catch up. "Hustle" is not an attribute often associated with older folks.

Loss of comfort level. Things were just fine when you knew how things worked and what was expected.

Paranoia. There's also a concern that people will make fun of you if you try something new and don't catch on quickly.

If an older person does not adapt, or react well to change, critics must be resistant to the notion that they've always been that way. Besides, septuagenarians, and people older than that, know something about change. They've lived it. Even more so than the kids of today.

They know about sacrifice when parents and loved ones went to war, and especially when they did not return. Then they went to war themselves and learned about jungle fighting. They know about the world entering the atomic age and the daily threat of nuclear annihilation.

They know about radio being elbowed out of the way by television, and black and white TV overcome by color.

They know about the transformative jet age.

They know about 35 millimeter cameras and Polaroid and cameras in phones.

They know about rockets reaching the moon and beyond.

They know about assassinated presidents and murdered civil rights leaders.

They know about disgrace in the White House.

And, they learned to call stewardesses "flight attendants."

Here are a few other things that popped up along the way. The microwave oven, mobile phones, Frisbees, slinkies, Velcro, credit cards, bar codes and scanners, microchips, transistor radios, optic fiber, the VCR, the ATM, the word processor, the Ethernet, Post-It notes, Walkman, IBM PC, Apple Macintosh, World Wide Web, digital cell phones, Viagra and Prozac. And so on. All of these things brought about change. They adjusted.

So, don't get up tight if they have not yet signed on to some of the changes in today's world that will only be around until the next best thing comes along.

Something does seem to happen later in life when we are reluctant to embrace change, and somehow actually come to fear it. It usually begins when we find ourselves saying, "They didn't do it that way when I was a kid." Or, "They don't make 'em like that anymore."

It's called nostalgia.

I suspect our fathers and grandfathers went through the same thing. No doubt there was some resistance to change for every generation. Who needs a refrigerator when the cold cellar is just fine? Who needs the automatic transmission when the stick shift gets you there too. Imagine what the makers of buggies and buggy whips were saying when the first automobiles hit the roads. Unpaved roads at that.

Almost fifty years ago, futurist Alvin Toffler wrote a book called *"Future Shock."* The basic premise was that the modern age brings significant change and brings it quickly. There is a psychological cost to the people trying to adjust to that change. Toffler says the loss of the familiar creates a kind of psychological shock. As people adjust, more changes create more shock, and many times, we do not respond well. Especially as we age and are set in our ways. There is nothing inherently wrong with this. It's kind of a post traumatic stress disorder, PTSD. We can't stop it. But that doesn't mean we have to accept it, much less want to accept it.

Case in point. The lesbian, gay, bisexual, transgender, or LGBT, movement is in full flower. The train has left the station, and there is no turning back. Same sex marriage and gender transition are part of today's new world. Books are written, movies are made, television sitcoms are produced, and all have found humor and compassion in them. Court rulings at the highest level have affirmed the lifestyles, I think it's safe to say young people have found acceptance much more readily than their parents and grandparents. Young people accept the new much more readily than the older generation. Remember, we were young once, too.

Too many oldsters just can't wrap their arms (perhaps the wrong phrase) around a group they are still quite comfortable in describing in less-than-nice terms.

The resistance to change is extremely pronounced in the area of race and ethnicity. Large numbers of people, led by older white men, just can't get on board with racial equality. In the half-century since the Civil Rights Act, those in the older generation, as well as in more recent generations have dug in. Words like "nigger" and "coon" continue to roll off their lips in today's world as easily as they have all of their lives. Despicable? Yes. But true. And burying our heads in the sand to this will not make it go away.

Our African-Americans citizens aren't lynched as once was the case. But they are still verbally eviscerated in some of the nicest, and not so nice, homes and neighborhoods in America by whites from all walks of life. Once again, people "set in their ways" are most likely to use the offending phrases.

Today, as of the writing of this book, the latest wave of hysteria focuses on immigrants and refugees who "are not like us," and referred to as "the other." They are looked upon as a threat and dangerous. They are called "towel heads" and "wetbacks" and "Spics." The use of such language in all of the cases above is never far below the surface in older, white America.

Maybe this is when we should take heed of younger, more accepting people. After all, we can learn from them, too.

This is not to say all seniors are racist or biased. I would, however, reference the 2016 presidential primary campaign, and the rhetoric from many Republican candidates. Political polling indicates clearly that a big chunk of the GOP right supports inflammatory, racist, and ethnically biased campaigns. As the polls show us, that support is led by older, white American men. That is not to say all Republicans fall into this category. But sadly, millions do.

Lest anyone think I'm saying this is the sole preserve of the GOP, let me be clear in saying that there are many Democrats who feel the same way. They're just doing it more quietly, or they're doing it privately, which in its own way, is just as disturbing as what the loudmouths on the right are expressing.

A word of warning for those whites who dislike, fear, or are suspicious of people of color. Within two or three decades, white Americans will be the nation's largest minority. The shoe will very likely be on the other foot. Careful, lest we be those that are thought to be lesser individuals.

Inflammatory, demeaning, and insulting language can be part of the problem when it comes to some of the other changes in recent history, too. Think about some of them and whether you've ever taken part in conversations like this.

- "Damn blacks have just come too far too fast." (You can substitute women and Hispanics for "blacks.")
- "Black lives don't matter when one of them's coming at you with a gun."

- "My God, if they legalize marijuana, the country will be overrun by junkies."
- "I don't want to watch television on a telephone. Phones are for making phone calls."
- "I want to hold a newspaper in my hand and not read it from a piece of plastic and glass." (You can substitute "book" for newspaper.)
- "When I started driving, gas was 15 cents a gallon."
- "When I started smoking, cigarettes were 15 cents a pack."
- "When I was a kid, movie tickets were 25 cents."
- "When I was a kid you could understand the words to a song, and hum the tune."
- Of course, that was back during "the good old days."

Many of today's elders look at today's world, the younger generation, and "the other" with a limited understanding of how and why it's working as it is. It's not "future shock." It's "present shock" and an inability to understand change and/or the speed of change. It has overtaken them. The minute they believe they are catching up, things change again, causing them to get angry and frustrated, longing ever more "for the good old days."

You remember the "good old days." Those were the days when there was no penicillin or Lipitor, cars overheated with regularity, there was no television, there was limited social justice, there was no Jennifer Lawrence. I just threw that in to see if you were paying attention.

Is it any wonder that today's younger people think that we are crabby, cranky, cantankerous, stubborn, and intolerant. They are not much interested in the way things used to be. They are more interested in what's happening now, and what's going to be. They will make of the future what they will. Just like we did.

Then they'll get older.

And they'll be just like us.

35: Sex

Last, but not least—or perhaps it is least—sex.

Let me begin by asking who wants a four-hour erection? Most boys and young men from age thirteen generally, until after the first year of marriage, experience something like the four-hour erection for much of the time during those years—without any assistance. Who wants to go back to those days when a sixteen year old would willingly hump a tree?

Most older men—much older men—would settle for a minute or two.

Two minutes seems like wishful thinking. More than that seems even more wishful. And erections are only part of the equation. Unless you are interested in sexual intercourse. Then of course one is faced with the problem of finding a partner. That may or may not work out just fine if the spouse is still alive. Again, I must point out that the approach to this subject comes from the male perspective. Then again, the fact that the spouse is still with us is not necessarily a guarantee that we are dealing with a willing partner. Remember those headaches when you were both in your thirties and had two or three, or more, kids down the hall? Those were the years of what we might call the "unrequited erection," sometimes known as the "migraine rejection."

Today's television talk and reality shows have no trouble talking about anything, much less about sexual activity among seniors. It is usually framed in the context that sexual drive and desire do not, or need not, diminish with age. But, just as the ability to drive a car well, or even at all, as the years advance, the sex drive seems to have something like an expiration date as well. It's not something that the kids can take away from you. It just seems that at some point, the sex drive goes out for a pack of cigarettes and does not come back.

The only action one can count on in bed in those older years is getting up in the middle of the night to take a pee. I want to issue extreme caution here. Be careful you don't knock down your wife as you go in, and she comes out, or vice versa. And this is most certainly happening after you have gone to bed at different times. She stays up to watch Jimmy Kimmel, or you tarry to watch an old movie. One or the other is sure to be sound asleep when the other comes to bed.

Until the need to take that pee.

This is not true for everyone I know, but many older men of my acquaintance seem to be satisfied with the heavy breathing on cable TV shows, wishing only that the shows had been available when they were teenagers. Especially at sixteen.

A Duke University study shows that only one in five people over the age of 65 continue to be happily, sexually active. If they take care of themselves, there's no reason older people can't have good sex until the end of their lives. Did you read that "until the end of their lives?" There's no mention in the study that the sexual activity may be the cause of the "end of their lives."

But, for the seniors who want to get back into the saddle, those heavily advertised little blue pills, or the others that those two people together in separate bathtubs (what's up with that?) use, can help the mister saddle up. The four-hour erection is the least of the problems for people of a certain age as you will see with a careful reading of the "Do not take VIAGRA (sildenafil citrate) if you …" that is displayed on the VIAGRA website. No chance in hell you can read the fine print at the bottom of the screen during their commercial.

Take a gander at their site. Those little blue pills offer a lot more than the possibility of a four-hour erection. And by the way, without a recent EKG, stress test, or attending physician, who could possibly answer the question, "Is your heart healthy enough for sex?" For what I assume is a large percentage of older guys, the default answer has to be "no." Better safe and horny, than sorry.

And you certainly noticed that it is possible that one can take the blue pills and wind up with a four-hour erection, and be blind and deaf at the same time. Not the best trifecta incentive for lovemaking.

It's just possible that one or more of the above medical conditions might apply to someone who is in the category we are discussing here, older gentlemen. I refer to the list that includes angina, irregular heartbeat, and/or high or low blood pressure. If none of these listed conditions apply to you, find a partner and go for it.

There are also embarrassment factors when it comes to all of this talk of erections and sex. One of them is asking the doctor for a prescription for the pills. The other is taking it to a pharmacist. Using a mail-order pharmacy can take care of the latter. Actually admitting to your doctor that you want to get laid can be problematic. Who among us would not fear the potential of an outburst of laughter from the physician, especially if he, or she, is younger. And, if it's a she? Well, you're a better man than I am if you have no problem dancing through this minefield. Perhaps they would laugh less if you walked in with one of those four-hour erections that refused to go away and may need to be taken care of surgically. I kid you not.

A few years ago, a friend of mine, a contemporary and a widower, wanted to give pleasure to his new girlfriend, but was having trouble doing so. She was a ready and impatient septuagenarian as was he, and he was interested in the little blue pills. But, he happened to be hard of hearing. When he asked my advice, I warned that it could cause a heart attack, which he apparently misheard as a "hard attack." That's exactly what he wanted to hear. A few days later he died in his girlfriend's bed after having had both a "hard" and "heart" attack.

All is not doom and gloom when it comes to sex after 65, 70 or 80. One does not run the risk of an unwanted pregnancy.

One thing that many older people don't think about today is STDs. Chances for contracting a sexually transmitted disease would seem remote. But that is not the case.

With the absence of a spouse, the issue of finding a partner becomes a critical one. Most of the rules that applied to swinging singles a few decades earlier are probably no longer valid.

Singles bars are interesting if for no other reason than to watch the dynamics of the place. Men firing on women. Women pretending to be coy, except for those actually and obviously firing on men. One can hear any number of lines that are used to stir up conversation. A couple I know that are tried and true, even after many years of use, and some might argue, years of abuse. "May I buy you a drink?" still has a lot traction. It has a reasonably good chance of breaking the ice with women. Men will never reject being offered a free drink whether there's a chance he'll score or not.

"What is your sign?" was an overture line that was used extensively in the seventies until it reached comic proportions. It was usually a line offered by men. You can still hear it occasionally, and it may still work from time to time. It can backfire, however, as women of the modern era will likely find it quite ridiculous. And there's always a chance they will consider it a portal to a possible follow up, such as "How old are you?" On the other hand, a few women might be interested in finding out what makes the guy who uses a bad thirty-year-old line, tick In today's world, one might have more success asking a young lady for her Twitter handle. Or, whether she has a Facebook page. Or is on Instagram.

Experience shows that a man's best chance at scoring is coming to the party in a BMW, wearing a Rolex, and sporting a cashmere jacket. That has as good a chance of getting a meaningful conversation going as anything. If a woman does not respond to the cashmere or Rolex, asking her, "Wanna see my BMW?" might just do it.

The older gentleman might have the jacket, car and Rolex, but he also has something else that can scotch the deal. Age. And, most of the real action takes place after the usual 9:30 bedtime. So, forget the traditional singles bar. The competition is too keen, and the women are not likely to go home with Daddy ... unless they are looking for a sugar daddy. Then she'll jump at the chance to see that BMW. As we all know, that is what some are looking for. But do you really want to go there? Next thing you know, they'll want to be put in your will, and likely have a man, again feeling his oats, thinking it was his idea. After that, they may try and kill you.

The best place to meet women that might respond to an older man's overtures is to go where they are. Unfortunately, most of them are in nursing homes or assisted living. You may find them at church. But can you still find your way to your old church?

Perhaps you can join your late (or ex) wife's book club. Problem with that is if you are on the little blue pill, you may be half blind, hard of hearing, and need to use a book, not to read, but to hide that four-hour erection.

The supermarket is sometimes a good spot. Do you have time to spend half a day squeezing oranges in the hope you can start up a conversation with some attractive woman of your vintage?

And then there's this. You can always get a greeter's job at Walmart. But if you have any class at all, you might be sorely disappointed at the prospects. Unless you are attracted by overweight women buying cookies and chips in bulk and dressed in colorful polyester. Not that all Walmart shoppers are like that, but still ... By the way, the aprons are not very good cover for that lingering erection.

If you are fortunate enough to belong to a country club you might find the pickings more to your liking than most places. Certainly better than Walmart. But in such a small circle, word gets around. There are few secrets. That narrows the necessary strategies and tactics enormously, limiting one's opportunities of playing the field. You'll also likely find yourself in competition with widowed golfing buddies who, like you, also gave up on the singles bar.

There is an option out there that seems to be increasingly attractive to older men and women, just as it is to their younger lonely/horny/desperate counterparts. I'm speaking, of course, of online dating sites.

The first thing one must do is learn how to use a computer. Chances remain high that you still don't know how. You can generally take a course at a local community college. Better yet, you can recruit a child or grandchild to help. But, don't tell them what you are up to. The grandkids won't give a damn, and may find it hilarious, but kids are known to share funny stuff with their parents. And their parents, your own children, will almost certainly disapprove. If they know you are looking for companionship, they will consider it a betrayal of their mother's memory. (Remember, I'm mostly talking about older men, here.) Even worse, they might begin to look for someone they think would be an acceptable 'friend.' This is fraught with potential unpleasantness and can lead to ruptured relationships with the kids, as well as the proposed companion, whom you probably already know. After all, the kids are most likely to draw upon your own, or their mother's friends, as the most acceptable company for you. Let's face it, how many old people are the kids likely to know outside of their own parents' social circle? And if that's where they're looking, you have probably already considered and rejected anyone who might be on their list.

So, the online dating site will probably work best. Work up a good narrative as to your likes and dislikes, and what you are looking for in a companion. You can be creative in what you say about yourself. Realize too, that whoever responds will most certainly have been creative themselves. You must be careful not to suggest something like saying you are a golf enthusiast. Especially if you hate the game or are bad at it. As sure as you mention a golf fixation, a highly desirable candidate will propose that you meet at a local golf course and get to know each other over eighteen holes. Game over!

Don't use a recent photo. Find a flattering photo of yourself from about ten years ago. You can also have a professional photo taken. Insist that the photographer use the most flattering lighting and Photoshop the hell out of it. If anyone snaps at the bait, but then seems disappointed with the "real" you, you can suggest that the picture was taken just before the death of your wife, or just before bypass surgery.

Don't be surprised at the number of online responses. There are lots of people in your boat. The unfortunate part is that most of them are probably men, even though the vast majority of the older population are women.

Another interesting reality is that older men are far more likely than older women to be interested in a relationship and far more likely to be interested in sex. Various studies indicate older men are about five times more likely than women to seek a relationship, find one, and have sex with a new partner. Bad news for the guys. The bullpen is not deep. On the other hand, men are five times more likely to remarry than their female counterparts, too.

With this imbalance, there is one other consideration that might be worth raising. More men are trolling the net than women. More men are interested in sex than women. Therefore, it stands to reason that you may receive some responses from gay or transgender people, or from someone in drag. If you have no problem with that, then go for it. If you do, don't say I didn't tell you.

Another option is Facebook. Put yourself out there. Friend as many people as you can muster. "Like" everybody and everything. Before you know it, you'll have all sorts of options. Facebook is less private than some dating sites. If that doesn't bother you, it might be the way to go. One thing to remember, though, is that others may not be as honest as you. Some friends have photos of other people, claim to be other people, or claim to be single. Some, yes, even on Facebook, are not looking for friendship. They're looking to relieve you of the money you have on hand. So, before hitting that accept button, look through their friends, peruse their "About" page. If they have no friends, or there is nothing about them, and they've just joined Facebook, be wary. Then hit the reject button. They'll never know.

Speed-dating events are popping up with regularity, too, it seems. That's when interested man and women move quickly from table to table in a large room, and spend a few minutes chatting before moving on. If they find someone they are attracted to, they can take or build a relationship from there. Or not. It's a fast-moving process in which one can get winded. Remember the old ticker.

And, if none of these ideas has any appeal, there's always the singles bar!

Even with all the cautionary notes, it is still certainly possible to have a loving, caring, and compassionate relationship. Even when the plumbing no longer works, or the fire goes out for whatever reason. Because when it does, it's not necessarily, and often isn't, the result of a loss of affection or even desire. Age certainly plays a role, but more often than not, so do health issues, especially the effects of medication, and even certain surgeries. It can all be embarrassing and even humiliating. But where there's real love, it needn't be.

36: And So, We've Come to the End

So what has all of this been about?

As Woody Allen said, "Eighty percent of success is showing up." If getting older can be considered a success, and it is given the alternative, it is the natural consequence of just "showing up." It is the process that begins the moment we enter this world and ends when we leave it. Like most everything we encounter, it comes with baggage and consequences. The baggage, in some cases luggage of steamer trunk proportions, is filled with regret, unrealized ambition, unattended relationships, things left unsaid.

You fill your trunk and I'll fill mine. Privately!

The consequences of aging are many and varied, many of which are addressed on the proceeding pages. They can be frivolous like liver spots, although I know many men and women who support an entire industry by buying creams and lotions to remove or hide them. But in the grand scheme of things, they are less consequential than, let's say, liver cancer.

The consequences of "just showing up," then sticking around for seven, eight, or nine decades, can be painful, and may include the loss of loved ones, the loss of dignity, or recognition of how so many people are willing to put older people at the margins of society, and their lives. We, those of my generation, would argue that the generations behind us are actually standing on our shoulders and are the beneficiaries of our accomplishments, of which there are many. In fairness, our failures, too.

For better or worse, we are responsible for the world as it is today. It can be argued that it is generally better than worse. But what's bad is really bad. So, it was when I was born and Adolph Hitler was marching into Austria, Poland, France, and beyond, and when Hirohito gave the thumbs up to Tojo and his crowd.

When that was dealt with, the time of crisis morphed into the Cold War, Korea, followed by the Vietnam War, which our government refused to ever call it a war, and the awfulness of the Mideast dilemma. As a kid, I might have wondered how we had gotten into such a mess. I suspect I spent more time being thankful for television, cars with fins, penicillin, and worrying more about pimples than nuclear fallout.

Today's younger generation may have difficulty swallowing that they are indeed standing on our shoulders of success. Perhaps we've earned that. The world was not a perfect place when I came into it. It's not perfect now, and it won't be perfect when I leave it. Actually, when any of us leave it. On the balance sheet, it's probably better now in most ways. Nonetheless, it becomes harder to think ill of those who may feel we have pretty much failed on making this a better place for them. So, I'll gladly pass the torch to them. Now, it's their turn to fix things. As the generation before me probably said, "Good luck with that."

We may have some regrets with the way we handled things, but at least some of the regrets are fixable. We can't fix unrealized ambition. But moping about it accomplishes nothing. Besides, as long as we are breathing, it is not too late to set new goals. We can volunteer, find new hobbies, spend more time with friends and grandkids. And don't sell short putting on a red apron at Walmart. It's someplace to go every day, or every once in a while, and it's a chance to interact with people.

If there are things that have been left unsaid, and the people to whom they were unsaid are still on this planet, there is still time to say them. Do it. It is therapeutic. And, if there is still a possibility to tend to relationships that you've let slide, that's an easy fix. Be it "I love you," "I'm sorry," or "I'm proud of you," all you have to do is say it. It costs nothing. Maybe that's another way to look at the expression, "Talk is cheap." Talk, too, can be rich in repairing relationships. Even if the other party chooses not to, you'll have the satisfaction of being the bigger person. Forgiveness, after all, frees you from the burden of carrying around that regret.

The bottom line, of course, is the bottom line. John Gunther, journalist and author of *Death Be Not Proud*, once wrote, "Live while you live, then die and be done with it." At the risk of being trite, it makes sense to make the most of all of one's years. When the "being done with it" time comes, one would not want to end it with disappointment, the way singer Peggy Lee describes in her wonderfully spoken song, *Is That All There Is?*

The song is about any number of life's occurrences, good and bad, and how they may or may not (usually not) live up to expectations. She's looking back and wondering right up to the final moment when she's about to draw her final breath, and asks for the last time, "Is that all there is?" (As with many oldies but goodies, Lee's song can still be heard on YouTube.)

How we live our lives determines how, or whether, we ask that same question. The time to be thinking about the question, and to avoid disappointment with the answer, is *now*, whatever your "now" happens to be.

Regardless of at what stage of the aging process you are, it is not a time for despair. Take a hint from the British facing one of the most dangerous, threatening, and hopeless periods in their history. Hitler was just across the channel. The blitz was on. Food was scarce. But the citizens were motivated by the omnipresent encouragement: Keep Calm and Carry On.

It worked for the Brits. It can work for us too.

I hope.

Post Script
(Well, I'll be damned!)

Okay, the best laid plans and all of that. Since sending this manuscript off to the publishers … and before a final edit … something has happened. A bad diagnosis.

Cancer!

Still furrows to plow to get it all sorted out, but it puts a lot of what has come before in some perspective (see Mortality).

I should preface what follows with a little perspective. My mother died of liver cancer, a cancer that had spread from her colon. She felt sick on Thanksgiving and was dead around Valentine's Day.

My father had cancer of his larynx. The cancer was removed, unfortunately, so was his larynx. He whispered his way to the end, which came in his sleep with a massive heart attack. No comfort to me, a man who has undergone a triple bypass and is dealing with AFib. My medicine cabinet rivals Walgreens.

My brother died of cancer of the bladder.

So, so much for the humor.

My particular problem is somewhat different. No one would ever wish for this particular disease in any form. Two strike me as particularly unwelcome; cancer of the brain or rectum. I got the rectum card.

There is something about that, it seems to me, that offers a dual response. Family and friends will groan in despair and perhaps even prayer. Then, from those somewhat further removed, the afflicted are more likely to become the "butt" of inevitable jokes, finding it hard to resist gallows humor when learning about the victim's malady: "I always thought he was an asshole." "Oh crap, not that!" "Who gives a shit!"

In full disclosure, I would have been in the wisecracking vanguard of this group.

We could go on and on. I'd rather not. My stomach aches from all the laughter.

Now that I have written the above words I await (I hate to use this phrase) a "final" determination of what the future will bring. Here's the timetable.

January 20

It unfolded thusly. Blood in the stool, a colonoscopy, and a couple of polyps removed. One's suspicious. A biopsy shows it to be malignant. It's gone, but? The question remains, does anything remain hidden behind the incision and the colon wall? A CT scan is clean, but doctors recommend surgery to be absolutely certain. It seems CT scans are not always reliable. Let's pick up the story from the biopsy of that tissue removed in mid-February. The pathologist received the tissue quite promptly.

<u>February 22</u>

I get a look online at the pathologist's findings. There's a little bit of something called … well … let's let the expert to spell it out … this is from an online (private, I hope) analysis of the biopsies.

"Sections of the rectal mass show well-differentiated adenocarcinoma, a portion of which shows an extensive mucinous component. The tumor is not noted at the proximal and distal inked margins of resection."

Comforting. Especially the "mass is not noted at the proximal and distal linked margins…."

Okay, sounds like the little cancer bugger is contained, which to my way of thinking, is a lot better than letting the intruder tour my body.

Then there's a line about the mass being *"unoriented."* That sounds positive. Or maybe not. Does that mean "disoriented?" It could be set for that "tour," but just uncertain about the destination. The only thing I am certain of is that it is not, apparently, going to the Orient. Is putting it that way even politically correct?

In the ever evident attempt to find positives in the

ocean of bad … this line stands out: *"No gross abnormalities are otherwise observed superficially."*

"*Superficially?*

Who the heck wants anything regarded superficially when we're talking about cancer and where superficial is not a wonderful diagnosis option when it comes to a disease that can do you in?

Okay, now back to the world where people who know the lingo get to interpret the official analysis of the biopsies. The good doctor makes the point. Cancer cells may be looking for a way out. The threat can be minimized by major surgery: a colostomy. Look it up. It would pain me too much to describe it. It's major. Chances of eliminating the threat are put at 97 - 99 percent. There are no sure things with cancer.

The other option is an MRI to see if the cells have escaped to rendezvous with lymph nodes. That's bad because it could enable the cells to hitch a ride to the liver, lungs, kidneys—or God forbid—the testicles.

What a one-two punch. Cancer of the rectum and/or testicles!

I'm going with the MRI. It's recommended that I wait six weeks until the fallout from the previous surgery is healed. Looking sooner might produce some disquieting false positives. Taking those MRI pictures too soon might show some tissue and lymph nodes still smarting from the surgery. We want a nice, clear, irrefutable picture. If it shows cells are on the move, we go to a lymph node ambush with radiation and chemo.

It is my understanding there is no good science on how effective either is in dealing with those pesky lymph nodes. Chances of success in this strategy are put at a little better than 80 percent.

That's the course I have chosen. When I mentioned to the doctor that I had decided on what I indelicately referred to as a "crap shoot" (99 vs 80 percent) my wife suggested that that was probably not the best term for what was going on. I apologized for what was probably a phrase that in all probability was not funny in the office of a doctor with his particular specialty. To his credit, he said I was actually speaking a language familiar to those in his particular discipline. Good for him.

So, the next step is the MRI. That's six weeks away. So, I will only add to this laugh fest when I hear in the next few weeks.

Stay tuned.

<u>April 4</u>
The MRI's been done. It took five hours—four and half in waiting rooms, and thirty minutes or so in the "tube."

April 6 (my wife's birthday, Happy birthday)
An appointment with the doctor who has been treating me. And, a decision. The MRI has shown three suspicious, but inconclusively so, lymph nodes. The options.

#1: major rectum surgery. That includes a major quality of life adjustment. Like who wants a shit bag on the hip?

#2: Get some radiation and chemo going. I was invited to confer with the "chemists" in this specialty to get some idea of what that all involves. The problem is, there is no clear indication that signals the lymph nodes are cancerous. So, does one want to go through all of that when the questionable lymph nodes may be benign?

No!

And, during the conversation about that option, there was a problem "aside" from my own doctor when he proposed that I confer with a specialist in radiation, and with one who is a specialist in chemotherapy. One, I was told, was reasonable and would give me the straight (dare I say it?) poop. The other was described as a "medical hammer" who saw every problem as a nail, and would go for a "maximum" approach. Comforting eh?

My doctor also had another observation. While those three suspicious lymph nodes were tiny, they were, he said, "lighting up." That could signify the presence of tiny tumors. Or, it could be residue inflammation from the earlier surgery. It was the anticipation, and even probability of fallout from the earlier surgery, that necessitated a wait of six weeks between the initial surgery and MRI. It had been seven weeks between the two, but there was some comfort in hearing that the lymph node situation might not signal tumors at all.

So, we come to the last option.

#3: Wait and see and do another MRI in three more months to see if there's any change, growth or movement. The suspicious critters, by the way, are about the size of the top of a ballpoint pen. It's hard to imagine something so small could become so potentially devastating.

I'm going with the "wait and see" to determine if anything is growing.

Back in three months. I hope!

<u>July 7</u>

The MRI of consequence.

Forty-five minutes of listening to NPR on headsets designed to offset the background noise of clinging and clanging through the MRI process. If you've never had the experience, and I hope you don't, although it's not *that* bad, it is noisy. The hard part comes later, waiting for the result.

For reasons of summer scheduling, I was not to get a read from the doctor for thirteen days. Now, if you want to know what a period of disquiet, more commonly described as fear is, take on the worry about having acquired a potentially fatal illness, offset only slightly by the possibility of being off the hook.

My doctor made it easier. He called me three days later (on our wedding anniversary by the way) to tell us the images were clear.

Thank God. Looks good. On to the next challenge of this challenging process of growing old.

As I said at the outset. Getting older isn't for the faint of heart.

Let's go to press.

Acknowledgments

This book could not have been attempted were it not for my wife Julie who helped with narrative ideas under the condition I not reveal which ones. Nor would it have been accomplished were it not for the opportunity to survive nearly eight decades, and for those who helped me do so. And, it would not have been attempted were it not for all the older people I have known and know who have provided the insight, humor, and, at times, the pathos which accompanies us all on "the journey."

Thanks for all the years. Don't stop now.

About the Author

Don Marsh has been an active and award winning print, radio, and television journalist for fifty-five years. He has written two books including, *Flash Frames*, a memoir of his journalism career, and *How to Be Rude … Politely*. He was inducted into the St. Louis Media Hall of Fame in 2013, and named "Media Person of the Year" by the St. Louis Press Club in 2015. He holds an honorary doctorate in Arts and Letters from the University of Missouri, St. Louis.

CPSIA information can be obtained
at www.ICGtesting.com
Printed in the USA
LVHW03s1129100818
586305LV00002B/2/P